782.81
So5f

65977

DATE DUE			
Nov 24 69	Dec 13 '76		
Oct 26 70	Mar 9 78		
Dec 18 70	Mar 20		
Jan 5 '71	May 22 78		
Jan 19 '71	Apr 22 '8		
Jan 25 '71	Mar 24 8		
Jan 28 '71	Mar 15 82		
Feb 3 '7	Apr 30 82		
Jan 25 '72			
Jul 2 '75			
Oct 11 '76			
GAYLORD M-2			PRINTED IN U.S.A.

Book by

BURT SHEVELOVE

and

LARRY GELBART

Music and Lyrics by

STEPHEN SONDHEIM

ILLUSTRATED WITH A DRAWING BY HIRSCHFELD
AND PHOTOGRAPHS

DODD, MEAD & COMPANY

New York 1963

A FUNNY THING HAPPENED ON THE WAY TO THE FORUM

A Musical Comedy Based on the Plays of Plautus

To and From
T. M. P.

Zero Mostel, Jack Gilford and David Burns in

"A Funny Thing Happened on the Way to the Forum"

AUTHORS' NOTE

This is a scenario for vaudevillians. There are many details omitted from the script. They are part of any comedian's bag of tricks. The double take, the mad walk, the sighs, the smirks, the stammerings. All these and more are intended to be supplied by the actor and, hopefully, the reader.

ILLUSTRATIONS

A Funny Thing Happened on the Way to the Forum was first presented by Harold Prince at the Alvin Theatre, New York City, N. Y., on May 8, 1962, with the following cast:

(*In order of appearance*)

PROLOGUS, *an actor*	Zero Mostel
THE PROTEANS. Eddie Phillips, George Reeder, David Evans	
SENEX, *an old man*	David Burns
DOMINA, *his wife*	Ruth Kobart
HERO, *his son*	Brian Davies
HYSTERIUM, *slave to Senex and Domina*	Jack Gilford
LYCUS, *a buyer and seller of courtesans*	John Carradine
PSEUDOLUS, *slave to Hero*	Zero Mostel
TINTINABULA, *a courtesan*	Roberta Keith
PANACEA, *a courtesan*	Lucienne Bridou
THE GEMINAE, *courtesans*	Lisa James, Judy Alexander
VIBRATA, *a courtesan*	Myrna White
GYMNASIA, *a courtesan*	Gloria Kristy
PHILIA, *a virgin*	Preshy Marker
ERRONIUS, *an old man*	Raymond Walburn
MILES GLORIOSUS, *a warrior*	Ronald Holgate

Production Directed by George Abbott
Choreography and Musical Staging by Jack Cole
Settings and Costumes by Tony Walton
Lighting by Jean Rosenthal
Musical Direction by Harold Hastings
Orchestrations by Irwin Kostal and Sid Ramin
Dance Music Arranged by Hal Schaefer

MUSICAL NUMBERS

ACT I

"Comedy Tonight" PROLOGUS, THE PROTEANS AND THE COMPANY

"Love, I Hear" HERO

"Free" PSEUDOLUS, HERO

"The House of Marcus Lycus" LYCUS, PSEUDOLUS AND THE COURTESANS

"Lovely" HERO, PHILIA

"Pretty Little Picture" PSEUDOLUS, HERO, PHILIA

"Everybody Ought to Have a Maid" SENEX, PSEUDOLUS, HYSTERIUM, LYCUS

"I'm Calm" HYSTERIUM

"Impossible" SENEX, HERO

"Bring Me My Bride" MILES, PSEUDOLUS, COURTESANS AND PROTEANS

ACT II

"That Dirty Old Man" DOMINA

"That'll Show Him" PHILIA

"Lovely" PSEUDOLUS, HYSTERIUM

Funeral Sequence and Dance PSEUDOLUS, MILES, COURTESANS AND PROTEANS

"Comedy Tonight" THE COMPANY

The time is two hundred years before the Christian era, a day in spring.

The place is a street in Rome in front of the houses of ERRONIUS, SENEX, AND LYCUS.

The action is continuous, with a single intermission.

ACT ONE

❦ ❦ ❦

(PROLOGUS *enters through curtain and salutes audience.*)

PROLOGUS. Playgoers, I bid you welcome. The theatre is a temple, and we are here to worship the gods of comedy and tragedy. Tonight I am pleased to announce a comedy. We shall employ every device we know in our desire to divert you.

(*Gestures to orchestra, sings.*)

Something familiar,
Something peculiar,
Something for everyone:
A comedy tonight!
Something appealing,
Something appalling,
Something for everyone:
A comedy tonight!
Nothing with kings,
Nothing with crowns.
Bring on the lovers, liars and clowns!
Old situations,
New complications,
Nothing portentous
Or polite;

17

Tragedy tomorrow,
Comedy tonight!

(*During the following,* HE *brings on the three* PROTEANS.)

Something convulsive,
Something repulsive,
Something for everyone:
A comedy tonight!
Something esthetic,

PROTEANS.
Something frenetic,

PROLOGUS.
Something for everyone:
A comedy tonight!

PROTEANS.
Nothing of gods,
Nothing of Fate.

PROLOGUS.
Weighty affairs will just have to wait.

PROTEANS.
Nothing that's formal,

PROLOGUS.
Nothing that's normal,

PROTEANS.
No recitations to recite!

ALL.
Open up the curtain!

(*The curtain parts halfway, then closes as if by accident,
causing confusion. After a moment, it reopens completely,
revealing a street in Rome. Stage center stands the house
of* SENEX; *on either side, the houses of* LYCUS *and* ER-
RONIUS. SENEX'S *house is hidden behind another curtain.*)

PROLOGUS.
  Comedy tonight!

  (*Speaks.*)

It all takes place on a street in Rome, around and about
these three houses. (*Indicates* ERRONIUS'S *house.*) First, the
house of Erronius, a befuddled old man abroad now in
search of his children, stolen in infancy by pirates. (*Sings.*)

Something for everyone:
A comedy tonight!

  (*The* PROTEANS *appear in the upper window of the house
  and pantomime.*)

Something erratic,
Something dramatic,
Something for everyone:
A comedy tonight!
Frenzy and frolic,
Strictly symbolic,
Something for everyone:
A comedy tonight!

(*Speaks, indicating* LYCUS'S *house.*) Second, the house of
Lycus, a buyer and seller of the flesh of beautiful women.
That's for those of you who have absolutely no interest in
pirates. (*Sings.*)

Something for everyone:
A comedy tonight!

  (PROTEANS *dance in front of the house; one of them disappears into the floor.* PROLOGUS *reacts, then continues,
  speaking.*)

Raise the curtain!

  (*Inner curtain drops into floor.*)

And finally, the house of Senex, who lives here with his wife
and son. Also in this house lives Pseudolus, slave to the son.

Pseudolus is probably my favorite character in the piece. A role of enormous variety and nuance, and played by an actor of such . . . let me put it this way . . . I play the part. (*Sings.*)

Anything you ask for:
Comedy tonight!

    (PROTEANS *re-enter.*)

And these are the Proteans, only three, yet they do the work of thirty. They are difficult to recognize in the many parts they play. Watch them closely.

    (PROTEANS *appear in and out of* SENEX'S *house in assorted costumes.*)

A proud Roman.
A patrician Roman.
A pretty Roman.
A Roman slave.
A Roman soldier.

    (PROTEAN *appears with crude wooden ladder.*)

A Roman ladder.

    (PROTEAN *enters, juggling.*)

Tremendous skill!

    (HE *juggles badly.* PROTEAN *enters.*)

Incredible versatility!

    (HE *fumbles in changing wigs.* PROTEAN *enters with gong.*)

And, above all, dignity!

    (HE *strikes gong, his skirt falls.*)

And now, the entire company!

    (THE COMPANY *enters from* SENEX'S *house.*)

ALL. (*Sing.*)
  Something familiar,
  Something peculiar,
  Something for everybody:
  Comedy tonight!

STAGE RIGHT.
  Something that's gaudy,

STAGE LEFT.
  Something that's bawdy,

PROLOGUS.
  Something for everybawdy:

ALL.
  Comedy tonight!

MILES.
  Nothing that's grim,

DOMINA.
  Nothing that's Greek!

PROLOGUS. (*Indicating* GYMNASIA.)
  She plays Medea later this week.

ALL.
  Stunning surprises,
  Cunning disguises,
  Hundreds of actors out of sight!

ERRONIUS.
  Pantaloons and tunics!

SENEX.
  Courtesans and eunuchs!

DOMINA.
  Funerals and chases!

LYCUS.
  Baritones and basses!

21

PHILIA.
Panderers!

HERO.
Philanderers!

HYSTERIUM.
Cupidity!

MILES.
Timidity!

LYCUS.
Mistakes!

ERRONIUS.
Fakes!

PHILIA.
Rhymes!

DOMINA.
Mimes!

PROLOGUS.
Tumblers!
Grumblers!
Fumblers!
Bumblers!

ALL.
No royal curse,
No Trojan horse,
And a happy ending, of course!
Goodness and badness,
Man in his madness:
This time it all turns out all right!
Tragedy tomorrow!
Comedy tonight!
(ALL *exit, except* PROLOGUS. HE *addresses the heavens.*)

22

PROLOGUS. Oh, Thespis, we place ourselves in your hands. (*To audience.*) The play begins. (*Exits.*)

(SENEX *enters from his house, calls.*)

SENEX. Slaves! (PROTEANS *enter from* SENEX'S *house, dressed as* SLAVES.) We are about to start our journey. My robe. (PROTEANS *place robe on him.*) My wreath. (PROTEANS *place wreath on his head.*)

DOMINA. (*Appearing in doorway of* SENEX'S *house.*) Senex!

SENEX. (*Frowns.*) My wife.

DOMINA. Slaves! Stop cringing and fetch the baggage!

PROTEANS. (*Exiting into* SENEX'S *house.*) Yes, yes, yes.

DOMINA. Senex, you are master of the house and no help at all. Where is Pseudolus? Where is Hysterium? Summon them! (SENEX *is about to speak,* DOMINA *calls out.*) Pseudolus! Hysterium!

(HYSTERIUM *enters from* SENEX'S *house. During following,* SENEX *drifts toward* LYCUS' *house.*)

HYSTERIUM. Ah, Madam, you called?

DOMINA. Yes, Hysterium.

HYSTERIUM. And I answered. Ever your humble. (*Kisses hem of her cape.*)

DOMINA. Have you prepared my potions?

HYSTERIUM. (*Holds up small bag.*) Yes, madam. In addition to your usual potions, I have included one for tantrums and one for queasiness.

DOMINA. Thank you, Hysterium, slave of slaves.

HYSTERIUM. I live to grovel. (*Kisses her hem.* DOMINA *calls to* HERO *on balcony of* SENEX'S *house.*)

23

DOMINA. Hero, come kiss your mother goodbye.

HERO. Yes, mother. (*Exits into* SENEX'S *house.* SLAVES *reenter, carrying baggage.*)

DOMINA. Slaves, take that baggage and go before us, you clumsies!

PROTEANS. (*As* THEY *scurry off.*) Yes, yes, clumsies, yes.

DOMINA. Senex! Come away from that house of shame!

SENEX. I was just standing here saying, "Shame, shame, shame!"

DOMINA. Hysterium!

HYSTERIUM. Yes, madam?

DOMINA. Where is Pseudolus?

HYSTERIUM. Where is he indeed! I have not seen him since he dressed Hero this morning.

DOMINA. Tell him that while we are gone, he is to watch over Hero. He is to keep him cheerful, well-fed, and far from the opposite sex.

SENEX. My dear, the boy has to learn sometime.

DOMINA. And when that time comes, *you* shall tell him . . .

SENEX. Yes, dear.

DOMINA. . . . what little you know. Now, go and fetch the gift we bring my mother.

SENEX. Yes, dear (*Exits into his house, as* HERO *enters from it.*)

HERO. Good morning, father.

DOMINA. Ah, Hero. Your father and I are off to visit my mother in the country. What a joy it would be were you

24

to accompany us. But, alas, the sight of anyone in good health fills my mother with rage. (SENEX *re-enters carrying a bust of* DOMINA.) Ah, there I am. Do you think it will please my mother?

HYSTERIUM. Oh, yes, madam. The craftsmanship is superb.

DOMINA. And the resemblance?

HYSTERIUM. Frightening.

DOMINA. The time of farewell is at hand. Hysterium, Slave-in-Chief, here are my husband's final instructions. (SENEX *opens his mouth to speak,* SHE *continues.*) In his absence, his entire household is in your spotless care. Your word shall be absolute, your authority unquestioned.

SENEX. And furthermore—

DOMINA. We are on our way!

SENEX. (*Mutters.*) We are on our way.

DOMINA. Farewell, beloved son. Farewell, thoughtful Hysterium. Senex, come along! And carry my bust with pride. (*Exits. A beat, and then her voice is heard.*) Senex!

SENEX. Yes, dear. (*To audience.*) A lesson for you all. Never fall in love during a total eclipse! (*Exits.*)

HYSTERIUM. (*To audience.*) Well, to work, to work! Now that I am completely in charge, I am going to be a very busy slave. (*Sees* HERO, *who has drifted toward* LYCUS' *house.*) Here! Come away from there. You must never know what goes on in that house.

HERO. But I do know.

HYSTERIUM. You do? (HERO *nods.*) Isn't it amazing? Well, I can't stand here talking. (*Goes to* SENEX'S *house, picks something from a column, stamps it out, grimaces, enters house, calling.*) Pseudolus!

(HERO *watches him go, then turns to audience.*)

HERO. (*Sings.*)
   Now that we're alone,
   May I tell you
   I've been feeling very strange?
   Either something's in the air
   Or else a change
   Is happening in me.
   I think I know the cause,
   I hope I know the cause.
   From everything I've heard,
   There's only one cause it can be . . .

   Love, I hear,
   Makes you sigh a lot.
   Also, love, I hear,
   Leaves you weak.

   Love, I hear,
   Makes you blush
   And turns you ashen.
   You try to speak with passion
   And squeak . . .
   I hear.

   Love, they say,
   Makes you pine away,
   But you pine away
   With an idiotic grin.
   I pine, I blush,
   I squeak, I squawk.
   Today I woke
   Too weak to walk.
   What's love, I hear,
   I feel . . . I fear . . .
   I'm in.

(*Sighs.*)

See what I mean?
Da-da-da-da-da-da-da . . .
(I hum a lot, too.)
I'm dazed, I'm pale,
I'm sick, I'm sore;
I've never felt so well before!
What's love, I hear,
I feel . . . I fear . . .
I know I am . . .
I'm sure . . . I mean . . .
I think . . . I trust . . .
I pray . . . I must . . .
Be in!
Forgive me if I shout . . .
Forgive me if I crow . . .
I've only just found out
And, well . . .
I thought you ought to know.

(PROTEANS *enter dressed as* CITIZENS, *holding* PSEUDO-LUS *by the arms.* THEY *utter obviously fake chatter.*)

HERO. Pseudolus!

FIRST CITIZEN. (*Salutes.*) Citizen! This is your slave? He was parading as a citizen.

PSEUDOLUS. Believe me, master, I was not parading. This is parading. (*Demonstrates.*) *I* was walking. (*Starts to walk off.* CITIZEN *stops him.*)

SECOND CITIZEN. Come back here!

THIRD CITIZEN. (*To* HERO.) He invited us to game with him, and, in a matter of moments, he had taken all our money.

FIRST CITIZEN. He was using weighted dice!

27

HERO. (*To* PSEUDOLUS.) Return the money.

SECOND CITIZEN. He took nine minae.

PSEUDOLUS. Nine?! I took seven!

HERO. Give them nine.

PSEUDOLUS. (*Handing coins to* CITIZEN.) One, two, three, four. I am being cheated out of the money I won fairly.

HERO. Pseudolus!

PSEUDOLUS. (*Giving* CITIZENS *coins.*) Seven, eight.

FIRST CITIZEN. What happened to five and six?

PSEUDOLUS. I'm coming to them. Nine, five, six! (*Hands them three more coins.*)

SECOND CITIZEN. Come, fellow citizens! (CITIZENS *exit, chattering.*)

PSEUDOLUS. (*Sheepishly.*) I should be whipped . . . gently. But I only did it for money. I thought if I could raise enough you'd let me buy my freedom from you.

HERO. Oh, Pseudolus, not again!

PSEUDOLUS. It's all I think about. I hate being a slave.

HERO. Better a slave than a slave to love.

PSEUDOLUS. That's easy for you to . . . Love? You? Tell me, master, who is she? Anyone I know?

HERO. Sometimes you can see her through that window. (*Points to* LYCUS' *house.*)

PSEUDOLUS. Through that win— (*Horrified.*) A courtesan in the house of Lycus? Your parents would be outraged if they could hear you.

HERO. I don't care!

PSEUDOLUS. Do you know how many minae a girl like that would cost?

HERO. And worth every drachma! Oh, Pseudolus, I would give anything for her.

PSEUDOLUS. You would? You really love this girl? (HERO *sighs.*) I like the way you said that. Now, you cannot afford to buy this girl, but in spite of that, suppose someone, someone with tremendous cunning and guile, could arrange for her to be yours.

HERO. Yes?

PSEUDOLUS. If that someone could arrange it, what would you give me?

HERO. Everything!

PSEUDOLUS. Everything? What do you own? Twenty minae, a collection of sea shells and me.

HERO. Right.

PSEUDOLUS. You don't have to give me the twenty minae, or the sea shells. If I get you that girl, just give me me.

HERO. Give you you?

PSEUDOLUS. My freedom.

HERO. Pseudolus! People do not go about freeing slaves.

PSEUDOLUS. Be the first! Start a fashion!

HERO. (*A pause, then:*) Get me that girl!

PSEUDOLUS. And if I can?

HERO. You are free!

PSEUDOLUS. I am what?

HERO. Free!

PSEUDOLUS. Free! (*Sings.*)
  Oh, what a word!
  Oh, what a word!
  (*Speaks.*) Say it again!

HERO. Free!

PSEUDOLUS. (*Sings.*)
  I've often thought,
  I've often dreamed
  How it would be . . .
  And yet I never thought I'd be . . .
  (*Speaks.*) Once more.

HERO. Free!

PSEUDOLUS. (*Sings.*)
  But when you come to think of such things . . .
  A man should have the rights that all others . . .
  Can you imagine
  What it will be like when I am . . .
  Can you see me?

  Can you see me as a Roman with my head unbowed?
  (Sing it good and loud . . .)

HERO.
  Free!

PSEUDOLUS.
  Like a Roman, having rights
  And like a Roman, proud!
  Can you see me?

HERO.
  I can see you!

PSEUDOLUS.
  Can you see me as a voter fighting graft and vice?
  (Sing it soft and nice . . .)

HERO.
Free.

PSEUDOLUS.
Why, I'll be so conscientious that I may vote twice!
Can you see me?
Can you see me?
When I'm free to be whatever I want to be,
Think what wonders I'll accomplish then!
When the master that I serve is me and just me,

Can you see me being equal with my countrymen?
Can you see me being Pseudolus the Citizen?
Can you see me being—? Give it to me once again!

HERO.
Free!

PSEUDOLUS.
That's it!

HERO.
Free!

PSEUDOLUS.
Yes!

HERO.
Fr . . .

PSEUDOLUS. (*Claps his hand over* HERO's *mouth.*)
Now, not so fast!
I didn't think . . .
The way I am,
I have a roof,
Three meals a day,
And I don't have to pay a thing . . .
I'm just a slave and everything's free.
If I were free,

31

Then nothing would be free,
And if I'm beaten now and then,
What does it matter?

HERO. (*Softly, seductively.*)
Free.

PSEUDOLUS. (*Brightening.*)
Can you see me?
Can you see me as a poet writing poetry?
All my verse will be . . .

HERO.
Free!

PSEUDOLUS.
A museum will have me pickled for posterity!
Can you see me?

HERO. (*With a grimace.*)
I can see you!

PSEUDOLUS.
Can you see me as a lover, one of great renown,
Women falling down?

HERO.
Free?

PSEUDOLUS.
No, but I'll buy the house of Lycus for my house in town.
Can you see me?
Can't you see me?
Be you anything from king to baker of cakes,
You're a vegetable unless you're free!
It's a little word but oh, the difference it makes:
It's the necessary essence of democracy,
It's the thing that every slave should have the right to be,
And I soon will have the right to buy a slave for me!

Can you see him?
Well, I'll free him!
When a Pseudolus can move, the universe shakes,
But I'll never move until I'm free!
Such a little word, but oh, the difference it makes:
I'll be Pseudolus the founder of a family,
I'll be Pseudolus the pillar of society,
I'll be Pseudolus the man if I can only be . . .

HERO.
Free!

PSEUDOLUS.
Sing it!

HERO.
Free!

PSEUDOLUS.
Spell it!

HERO.
F-r-double . . .

PSEUDOLUS.
No, the long way . . .

HERO.
F-R-E-E-

BOTH.
FREE!!!

(LYCUS *enters from his house, calls into it.*)

LYCUS. What a day! What a day! Come out here! (PROTEAN, *dressed as* EUNUCH, *enters from house, holding fan.*) What do you think you are doing, eunuch? I have told you a thousand times not to fan the girls while they're still wet! You'll never learn. You'll be a eunuch all your life! (EUNUCH *exits into house.* LYCUS *turns to audience.*) What a day! I have to go to the Senate this morning. I'm blackmailing one of the Senators. (*Starts off, as* PSEUDOLUS *whispers to* HERO.)

PSEUDOLUS. Quick! Your money bag! (HERO *hands him money bag.*) Good morning, Lycus. (*Jingles money bag behind* LYCUS' *back.* LYCUS *stops.*)

LYCUS. I know that sound, and I love it. (*Turns to* PSEUDOLUS.) Is that money?

PSEUDOLUS. What do you think?

LYCUS. How did you come to all this?

PSEUDOLUS. An unexpected legacy. My uncle Simo, the noted Carthaginian elephant breeder, came to an untimely end. He was crushed to death on the last day of the mating season. This morning I bought my freedom.

LYCUS. Congratulations!

PSEUDOLUS. With this much left over for one gross indulgence.

LYCUS. Good.

PSEUDOLUS. Lycus, I am now in the market for a lifetime companion. Tell me, have you anything lying about in there, anything to satisfy an Olympian appetite?

LYCUS. Pseudolus, friend and *citizen,* I have traveled the world in search of beauty, and I can say with modesty that I have the finest assortment in Rome.

PSEUDOLUS. Show me.
 (LYCUS *claps his hands.*)

LYCUS. Eunuchs! A buyer!

 (EUNUCHS *enter from* LYCUS' *house, drape banner over door.* PSEUDOLUS *sits on stool.* LYCUS *sings.*)

34

There is merchandise for every need
At the house of Marcus Lycus.
All the merchandise is guaranteed
At the house of Marcus Lycus.
For a sense of sensuality
Or an opulence thereof,
Patronize the house of Marcus Lycus,
Merchant of love.

For your most assured approval and your more than possible purchase, here are the fruits of my search. Behold . . . Tintinabula. (TINTINABULA *enters from behind banner, poses.*) Out of the East, with the face of an idol . . . the arms of a willow tree . . . and the pelvis of a camel.

(SHE *dances.* PSEUDOLUS *looks at* HERO, *who shakes his head "no."*)

PSEUDOLUS. (*To* LYCUS.) Don't you have anyone in there a bit less . . . noisy?

LYCUS. I have. May I present Panacea. (PANACEA *enters.*) To make her available to you, I outbid the King of Nubia. Panacea, with a face that holds a thousand promises, and a body that stands behind each promise.

(PANACEA *dances.* HERO *shakes his head "no."* PSEUDOLUS *looks* PANACEA *over, yawns.*)

You are disturbed?

PSEUDOLUS. The proportions. Don't misunderstand me. (*Spreading his hands before her bosom.*) I love the breadth. It's the length. She may be the right length, but is it right for me? You see what I mean. (*Stands with her, back-to-back.*) Isn't she a bit too short?

LYCUS. Definitely not.

PSEUDOLUS. (*Wiggles, then:*) Too tall?

LYCUS. No. Like that you look perfect together.

PSEUDOLUS. Yes, but how often will we find ourselves in this position? (*Turns to face her.*) Perhaps if we . . .

LYCUS. No need to compromise. Consider the Geminae. (*Geminae enter.*) A matched pair. (THEY *dance.*) Either one a divinely assembled woman, together an infinite number of mathematical possibilities. They are flawless. (HERO *shakes his head "no."*)

PSEUDOLUS. I quite agree. But I am a man of limited means and I don't suppose you'd break up a set.

LYCUS. I couldn't. You understand.

PSEUDOLUS. Completely.

LYCUS. Fortunately, we still have . . . Vibrata. (VIBRATA *enters.*) Exotic as a desert bloom . . . wonderous as a flamingo . . . lithe as a tigress . . . for the man whose interest is wild life . . .

> (VIBRATA *sings, dances.* HERO *shakes his head "no."* PSEUDOLUS *goes to* VIBRATA.)

PSEUDOLUS. Lycus, all that I can see is a sight to behold, but I keep feeling there is something wrong. Perhaps a cleft palate, a hammer toe . . .

LYCUS. Wait. I know exactly what you want. May I present . . . Gymnasia. (GYMNASIA *enters, does bump.* PSEUDOLUS *falls off stool.* HERO *shakes his head "no," but* PSEUDOLUS *is completely captivated.*) Gymnasia, a giant stage on which a thousand dramas can be played.

> (PSEUDOLUS *circles her, stops behind her, gestures to* LYCUS.)

PSEUDOLUS. Lycus, could I see you back here a moment? (LYCUS *disappears behind* GYMNASIA. HE *and* PSEUDOLUS *gesture.* PSEUDOLUS *steps into the clear.*) Two hundred minae?! For what?!

LYCUS. Figure it out for yourself.

PSEUDOLUS. Yes, it is a fair price by the pound. But what disturbs me, frankly, is the upkeep. Perhaps you would have more success selling her to some fraternal organization. A group dedicated to good works. But on the other hand . . . (*Puts his head on her bosom.*)

HERO. Pseudolus!

PSEUDOLUS. Yes, darling?

HERO. (*Pulls him aside.*) Do you want your freedom?

PSEUDOLUS. (*Looks back at* GYMNASIA.) More than ever. (*To* LYCUS.) May I see the next girl?

LYCUS. That is the entire lot. Surely there is one among these to satisfy you.

PSEUDOLUS. As yet I have not seen exactly what I had in mind.

LYCUS. (*Claps hands.*) Courtesans! Out of the sun and into the house. I shall return in time to lead you in midday prayers.

(COURTESANS *and* EUNUCHS *exit.* PHILIA'S *head appears in upper window of* LYCUS' *house.*)

HERO. (*Whispers to* PSEUDOLUS.) Pseudolus, there she is!

PSEUDOLUS. (*To* LYCUS.) Oh, you fox! "That is the entire lot." Did I not just spy a golden head and a pair of sky blue eyes? A body clad in flowing white?

LYCUS. Oh, that one. A recent arrival from Crete. A virgin.

PSEUDOLUS. (*Nudging* HERO.) A virgin.

HERO. A virgin!

PSEUDOLUS. (*To* LYCUS.) Well??

LYCUS. Only yesterday she was sold.

HERO. Sold! (*Draws his dagger melodramatically.* PSEUDOLUS *wrests it from him.*)

PSEUDOLUS. Behave yourself! (*Begins casually cleaning his nails with dagger.*) She was sold?

LYCUS. To the great captain, Miles Gloriosus, who comes this day to claim her. She cost 500 minae.

PSEUDOLUS. (*Amazed.*) Five hundred!

LYCUS. A great sum, to be sure. But being a man of conquest, his heart was set on a virgin.

PSEUDOLUS. You say she just arrived from Crete?

LYCUS. Yes.

PSEUDOLUS. Mmm. I hope the great captain is kind to her. She deserves a bit of affection before . . . (*Sighs, then to* HERO.) Tragic, is it not? (HERO *moans.*)

LYCUS. What is tragic?

PSEUDOLUS. The news from Crete.

LYCUS. What news?

PSEUDOLUS. Why should I darken your day? Farewell, Lycus.

LYCUS. (*Grabs him.*) What is the news?

PSEUDOLUS. What news?

LYCUS. The news from Crete.

PSEUDOLUS. I heard it. Tragic.

LYCUS. Pseudolus!

PSEUDOLUS. You force me to tell you! Crete is ravaged by a great plague. People are dying by the thousands.

LYCUS. But this girl is healthy. She goes smiling through the day.

PSEUDOLUS. She doesn't! I thought you knew. When they start to smile, the end is near.

LYCUS. No!

PSEUDOLUS. Yes. I am told it is lovely now in Crete. Everyone lying there, smiling.

LYCUS. Is it contagious?

PSEUDOLUS. Did you ever see a plague that wasn't?

LYCUS. My other girls!

PSEUDOLUS. You had best get her out of there.

HERO. Yes!

LYCUS. And then?

PSEUDOLUS. I could look after her until the captain comes.

HERO. He could!

LYCUS. But would *you* not be . . . ?

PSEUDOLUS. I have already had the plague. I would tell you about it but . . . (*Pantomimes disgust.*)

LYCUS. I do hope she lives until the captain gets here. (*Exits into his house.*)

HERO. Pseudolus, I am to be with her!

PSEUDOLUS. Until the captain arrives.

HERO. (*Sadly.*) Yes.

PSEUDOLUS. Wait! (*Thinks a moment.*)

HERO. Yes?

PSEUDOLUS. A brilliant idea!

HERO. Yes?

PSEUDOLUS. That's what we have to find. A brilliant idea.

(LYCUS *speaks into his house, as* HE *backs out of it.*)

LYCUS. Come, come, my dear. This way. Don't touch that pillar. Here is someone I want you to meet. (PHILIA *enters, carrying a bag.*) Philia, this is Pseudolus. You are to stay with him until the captain comes. It will not be long. (*Aside to* PSEUDOLUS.) Pseudolus! Thank you, Pseudolus. If none in the house were to your liking, there will soon be new arrivals. You shall have first choice, because, Pseudolus, you are a friend. (*Bows.*)

PSEUDOLUS. (*Returning the bow.*) And you, Lycus, are a gentleman and a procurer. (LYCUS *exits.* HERO *and* PHILIA *stand staring at each other.* PSEUDOLUS *looks at them, then turns to audience.*) There they are. Together. And I must keep them that way, together, if I am to be free. What to do? What to do? (*To himself.*) I need help. I'll go to the harbor. I am off! The captain! (HERO *and* PHILIA *turn to him, alarmed.*) Watch for him. He may arrive this way . . . (PHILIA *turns from* HERO, *looks off.*) . . . or he may arrive this way. (HERO *turns, looks off.*) No, no. You watch this way. (*Turns* PHILIA *around.*) And you watch that way. (*Turns* HERO *around.* HERO *and* PHILIA *now face each other.*) Much better. (*Starts to exit, stops, addresses audience.*) Don't worry. Nothing will happen. He's a virgin, too. (*Runs off.*)

PHILIA. My name is Philia.

HERO. Yes.

40

PHILIA. I do not know your name, but you have beautiful legs.

HERO. My name is Hero and . . . uh . . . you have beautiful legs . . . I imagine.

PHILIA. I would show them to you, but they are sold.

HERO. I know.

PHILIA. Along with the rest of me. I cost 500 minae. Is that a lot of money?

HERO. Oh, yes.

PHILIA. More than 300?

HERO. Nearly twice as much.

PHILIA. Those are the two numbers that mix me up, three and five. I hope that captain doesn't expect me to do a lot of adding.

HERO. You can't add?

PHILIA. We are taught beauty and grace, and no more. I cannot add, or spell, or anything. I have but one talent. (*Sings.*)

I'm lovely,
All I am is lovely,
Lovely is the one thing I can do.
Winsome,
What I am is winsome,
Radiant as in some
Dream come true.
Oh,
Isn't it a shame?
I can neither sew
Nor cook nor read nor write my name.
But I'm happy

Merely being lovely,
For it's one thing I can give to you.

HERO. Philia . . .

PHILIA. Yes?

HERO. Say my name.

PHILIA. Just say your name?

HERO. Yes.

PHILIA. Very well. (*A blank look.*) I have forgotten it.

HERO. (*Disappointed.*) It's Hero.

PHILIA. Forgive me, Hero. I have no memory for names.

HERO. You don't need one. You don't need anything. (*Sings.*)

You're lovely,
Absolutely lovely,
Who'd believe the loveliness of you?
Winsome,
Sweet and warm and winsome,
Radiant as in some
Dream come true.
Now
Venus would seem tame,
Helen and her thou-
Sand ships would have to die of shame.

BOTH.

And I'm happy,
Happy that you're (I'm) lovely,
For there's one thing loveliness can do:
It's a gift for me to share with you!

(THEY *kiss.*)

HERO. Do you know? I've never been kissed before.

PHILIA. That's the very first thing they teach us.

HERO. Philia . . . I love you.

PHILIA. And I love you.

(THEY *embrace, as* HYSTERIUM *enters from* SENEX'S *house, muttering.*)

HYSTERIUM. Pseudolus! Where is that—? (*Sees* HERO *and* PHILIA.) Oh, no! No, no, no, no!

HERO. Hysterium, this is Philia.

HYSTERIUM. Never mind who she is, who is she? Where is she from?

HERO. (*Haltingly.*) She is from the house of Lycus.

HYSTERIUM. A courtesan!

PHILIA. I am a virgin.

HYSTERIUM. (*With a fake smile.*) Of course. Hero, this will never do. Never, never. Bid farewell to this young lady so that she can go about her . . . uh . . . business.

HERO. But Pseudolus said . . .

HYSTERIUM. Pseudolus! I might have known!

(PSEUDOLUS *runs on.*)

PSEUDOLUS. Hero!

HYSTERIUM. Pseudolus! (PSEUDOLUS *reacts, polishes pillar of house.*) Pseudolus!

PSEUDOLUS. Yes, Hysterium?

HYSTERIUM. Pseudolus!

PSEUDOLUS. Pronounced perfectly! You know, a lot of people say *P*seudolus, and I hate it. (*Aside to* HERO.) Show the girl our garden.

43

(HERO *and* PHILIA *exit behind* SENEX'S *house.*)

HYSTERIUM. How dare you! Arranging an assignation between an innocent boy and a you-know-what!

PSEUDOLUS. Hysterium, there is something you should know about that you-know-what.

HYSTERIUM. What?

PSEUDOLUS. That girl, about whom you think the worst, is my daughter.

HYSTERIUM. Your what?

PSEUDOLUS. My daughter. You've heard me speak of her.

HYSTERIUM. Never!

PSEUDOLUS. Well, I don't like to talk about her. (*Polishes pillar.*)

HYSTERIUM. That girl is not your daughter.

PSEUDOLUS. My sister?

HYSTERIUM. I shall go tell his parents.

PSEUDOLUS. Wait! Hysterium, the truth. She has been sold to a captain who comes any moment now to claim her.

HYSTERIUM. Oh. I go tell his parents!

PSEUDOLUS. I go with you!

HYSTERIUM. You don't want to be there when I tell them about you!

PSEUDOLUS. No, I want *you* to be there when I tell them about *you!*

HYSTERIUM. Tell them *what* about me? I have nothing to fear. I am a pillar of virtue. I go. (*Starts to leave.*)

44

PSEUDOLUS. I think it might be of interest to the family that their slave-in-chief, their pillar of virtue, has secreted within the confines of his cubicle Rome's most extensive and diversified collection of erotic pottery.

(HYSTERIUM *freezes in horror.*)

HYSTERIUM. Pseudolus! (*Calls out.*) Hero!

PSEUDOLUS. Tell me, where did you ever get that fruit bowl with the frieze of . . . ? (*Indicates an erotic pose or two.*)

HYSTERIUM. Pseudolus!

(HERO *and* PHILIA *enter.*)

HYSTERIUM. Hero, as you know, your mother and father placed me in charge of your innocence. However, I have decided to allow you to remain with the girl until the arrival of her captain.

HERO. Oh, Philia! (*Embraces her.*)

HYSTERIUM. Here! Stop doing that! (*Separates them.*) You could hurt each other! (*Exiting into* SENEX'S *house.*) Ohhhhh!

PSEUDOLUS. Master, I said we needed a brilliant idea.

HERO. Yes?

PSEUDOLUS. I have been to the harbor, and I have found one. Come along!

PHILIA. Are we going somewhere?

PSEUDOLUS. *You* are. You have your belongings. (*To* HERO.) Let us fetch yours.

HERO. Where are we to go?

PSEUDOLUS. Away.

HERO. *Where* away?

PSEUDOLUS. *Far* away!

HERO. But my family . . .

PHILIA. My captain . . .

PSEUDOLUS. There is only room for two of you.

HERO. Where?

PSEUDOLUS. (*Sings.*)
In the Tiber there sits a boat,
Gently dipping its bow,
Trim and tidy and built to float.
Pretty little picture?
Now . . .
Put a boy on the starboard side,
Leaning out at the rail.
Next to him put a blushing bride,
Slim and slender and starry-eyed.
Down below put a tiny bed.
The sun gets pale,
The sea gets red,
And off they sail
On the first high tide,
The boat and the bed and the boy and the bride!

It's a pretty little picture, oh, my!
Pretty little picture, how true!
Pretty little picture which I,
Pseudolittlelus, give to you!

Feel the roll of the playful waves!
See the sails as they swell!
Hear the whips on the galley slaves!
Pretty little picture?
Well . . .
Let it carry your cares away,
Out of sight, out of mind,

Past the buoy and through the bay—
Soon there's nothing but sea and spray.
Night descends and the moon's aglow.
Your arms entwined,
You steal below,
And far behind
At the edge of day,
The bong of the bell of the buoy in the bay,
And the boat and the boy and the bride are away!

It's a pretty little picture to share
As the little boat sails to sea.
Take a little trip free as air,
Have a little freedom on me!

HERO and PHILIA.
No worries,
No bothers,
No captains,
No fathers!

PSEUDOLUS.
In the ocean an island waits,
Smooth and sandy and pink,
Filled with lemons and nuts and dates.
Pretty little picture?
Think:
In a cottage of cypress trees,
Sea-shells dotting the door,
Boy and bride live a life of ease,
Doing nothing but what they please.
And every night when the stars appear,
There's nothing more
To see or hear,
There's just the shore
Where the lovers lie,

The sand and the sea and the stars and the sky,
And the sound of a soft little satisfied sigh . . .

(HERO *and* PHILIA *sigh.*)

ALL.
All your petty little problems will cease,
And your little blessings will flow,
And your little family increase.
Pretty little picture?

PSEUDOLUS.
No, no!
Pretty little masterpiece!

ALL.
Pretty little picture!

PSEUDOLUS. Come! We go!

HERO. Yes!

PHILIA. Wait! I cannot go.

PSEUDOLUS. Why can you not?!

PHILIA. As long as the captain has a contract I must go with him. That is the way of a courtesan.

HERO. Oh, Venus, why did you bring us together, only to part us?

PHILIA. Be brave, Hero.

HERO. For us there will never be happiness.

PHILIA. We will have to learn to be happy without it.

PSEUDOLUS. (*To audience.*) Have you been listening? Do you believe this? And not a word about me or my freedom. (*Firmly.*) She *must* go with him!

PHILIA. This waiting out here is torture. Why doesn't he come and take me?

"Playgoers, I bid you welcome."
Zero Mostel as Prologus

Friedman-Abeles

DOMINA. "The time of farewell is at hand."
Domina (Ruth Kobart), Hysterium (Jack Gilford) and Senex (David Burns)

Van Williams

LYCUS. "May I present Panacea. To make her available
to you, I outbid the King of Nubia."
Lycus (John Carradine) and Panacea (Lucienne Bridou)

Van Williams

Friedman-Abeles

PSEUDOLUS. "Isn't she a bit too short?"
Panacea (Lucienne Bridou) and Pseudolus (Zero Mostel)

ERRONIUS. "My house is haunted, you say?"
Erronius (Raymond Walburn) and Hysterium (Jack Gilford)

"A giant stage on which a thousand dramas can be played"
Gloria Kristy as Gymnasia

SENEX. "My slave has prepared a little feast. I want you to serve it to me in there." Hysterium (Jack Gilford) and Senex (David Burr

Van Williams

PSEUDOLUS. "And not a word about me or my freedom." Hero (Brian Davies), Philia (Preshy Marker) and Pseudolus (Zero Mostel)

MILES. "All Crete was at her feet."

Pseudolus (Zero Mostel), Hysterium (Jack Gilford) and Miles (Ronald Holgate)

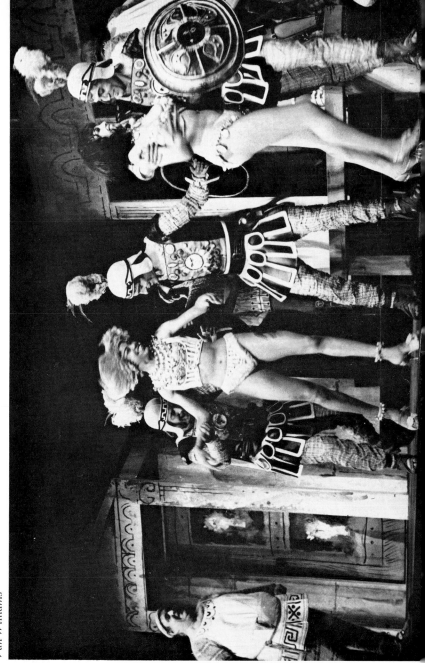

SOLDIERS. "We get a few girls."

Van Williams

"Comedy tonight!"

PSEUDOLUS. In good time you will be taken. But not on the street. Inside.

PHILIA. You will tell me when he comes?

PSEUDOLUS. I shall have him knock. On the door. Three times.

PHILIA. That's two and one more?

PSEUDOLUS. Correct. Three times. Now, in, in, in.

(PHILIA *exits into* SENEX'S *house.*)

HERO. (*Despondently.*) Pseudolus.

PSEUDOLUS. (*Confidently.*) She will go with you.

(HYSTERIUM *enters from* SENEX'S *house.*)

HYSTERIUM. Hero, I am off to market. While you are alone with the girl, remember who you are. (HERO *exits into* SENEX'S *house.*) I have yet to begin my daily chores.

PSEUDOLUS. Hysterium, before you go. Just one more favor.

HYSTERIUM. What is it?

PSEUDOLUS. May I borrow your book of potions?

HYSTERIUM. Oh, no, no, no! That stays right here . . . (*Pats his back pocket.*) Where it belongs. (*Calls off.*) You there, bird seller! What do you have in the way of a plump peahen? (*As* HE *exits,* PSEUDOLUS *deftly lifts potion book from* HYSTERIUM'S *back pocket, addresses audience.*)

PSEUDOLUS. His book of potions! And my pass to freedom! What I need is his sleeping potion. With a drop or two of that, the breath stops short, the eyes slam shut, the body hangs limp. I shall mix a few drops in a beaker of wine and give it to the girl to drink. I show Lycus that she has died of the plague and tell Hero to dispose of the body. Then they to the boat, I to the hills, (*Points to audience.*) and you to your homes. (*Looks through pages, then:*) I just

49

remembered something frightening. I cannot read! (*Calls.*) Hero! Come out here. (HERO *enters from* SENEX'S *house.*) Call these pages off to me.

HERO. Not now?!

PSEUDOLUS. Yes, now! Read!

HERO. (*Reading as* HE *turns pages.*) "Fever Potion" . . . "Headache Potion" . . . "Passion Potion" . . . "Sleeping Potion" . . .

PSEUDOLUS. That's it! The formula. What do we need? The ingredients?

HERO. "The eye of an eel."

PSEUDOLUS. That we have.

HERO. "The heart of a snail."

PSEUDOLUS. That we have.

HERO. "A cup of mare's sweat."

PSEUDOLUS. Mare's sweat? That we have not.

HERO. Why are you preparing this?

PSEUDOLUS. I intend to give it to the girl. Asleep, she will go with you.

HERO. She will?

PSEUDOLUS. (*Worried.*) Mare's sweat . . .

HERO. Where will you find it?

PSEUDOLUS. Leave that to me. *You* go to the harbor! Give the boatman your twenty minae and tell him that you sail with him this day! *I* shall prepare the potion!

HERO. This is exciting!

PSEUDOLUS. Isn't it? Go! (HERO *exits.*) Mare's sweat! Where am I going to find mare's sweat on a balmy day like this? (PSEUDOLUS *exits, as* SENEX *enters with* DOMINA'S *bust, calling.*)

SENEX. Pseudolus! Pseudolus! . . . He could have taken this to the stonecutter for me. (*To audience.*) I dropped it, and now the nose has to be re-sharpened. Hysterium will take it for me. (*Goes to his house, kicks door three times. A pause, then* PHILIA *enters from house, arms outstretched.*)

PHILIA. Take me! (SENEX *looks around.*) Take me!

SENEX. What did you say?

PHILIA. Take me!

SENEX. One moment. (*Puts statue on stoop, starts for* PHILIA, *returns to statue, and turns its face away from* PHILIA.)

PHILIA. Here on the street if you like! My body is yours. Say it. Say it!

SENEX. (*Looks around, then quickly.*) Your body is mine.

PHILIA. Then take me! (*Throws herself at him.*) Is this not what you want?

SENEX. It does cross my mind now and then.

PHILIA. You must know one thing.

SENEX. What is that?

PHILIA. Though you have my body, you shall never have my heart.

SENEX. Well, you can't have everything. (*Looks heavenward.*) A thousand thanks, whichever one of you did this. (SHE *seizes him.* THEY *hold their embrace as* PSEUDOLUS *enters, carrying a vial. Not seeing* SENEX *and* PHILIA, HE *addresses audience.*)

PSEUDOLUS. Would you believe it? There was a mare sweating not two streets from here. (*Holds up vial, turns, sees embrace.* SENEX'S *face is hidden from him.* PSEUDOLUS *turns to audience.*) Gets to look more like his father every day!

PHILIA. (*Still in* SENEX'S *arms.*) Pseudolus, he is here.

PSEUDOLUS. No!

(SENEX *looks from* PHILIA *to* PSEUDOLUS, *then back to* PHILIA.)

SENEX. Remember where we stopped. (*Slips out from under her, goes to* PSEUDOLUS.)

PSEUDOLUS. Sir, you're back.

SENEX. (*Holding his spine.*) She almost broke it.

PSEUDOLUS. You've returned!

SENEX. Yes!

PSEUDOLUS. Unexpectedly!

SENEX. Apparently! Who is she?

PHILIA. I shall await your bidding.

SENEX. Yes, dear.

PHILIA. Ever your servant. (*Bows, exits into* SENEX'S *house.*)

SENEX. (*Sighs.*) Ever my servant.

PSEUDOLUS. (*Quickly.*) Yes, sir. Your servant. Your new maid. We needed someone to help.

SENEX. A new maid. She seems very loyal.

PSEUDOLUS. And very efficient and very courteous and very thoughtful.

SENEX. Maids like me. I'm neat. I like maids. *They're* neat. Something no household should be without. (*Sings*, PSEUDOLUS *all the while encouraging him*.)

Everybody ought to have a maid.
Everybody ought to have a working girl.
Everybody ought to have a lurking girl
To putter around the house.

Everybody ought to have a maid.
Everybody ought to have a menial,
Consistently congenial
And quieter than a mouse.

Oh! Oh! Wouldn't she be delicious,
Tidying up the dishes,
Neat as a pin?
Oh! Oh! Wouldn't she be delightful,
Sweeping out, sleeping in?

Everybody ought to have a maid!
Someone whom you hire when you're short of help
To offer you the sort of help
You never get from a spouse!
Fluttering up the stairway,
Shuttering up the windows,
Cluttering up the bedroom,
Buttering up the master,
Puttering all around
The house!

(PSEUDOLUS *pantomimes a maid*.)

Oh! Oh! Wouldn't she be delicious,
Tidying up the dishes,
Neat as a pin?
Oh! Oh! Wouldn't she be delightful,
Sweeping out, sleeping in?

Everybody ought to have a maid!

Someone who, when fetching you your slipper, will
Be winsome as a whippoorwill
And graceful as a grouse!
Skittering down the hallway,
Flittering through the parlor,
Tittering in the pantry,
Littering up the bedroom,
Puttering all around
The house!

(HYSTERIUM *enters, reacts at the sight of* SENEX. PSEU-
DOLUS *whispers to him.*)

HYSTERIUM. A maid?

PSEUDOLUS. A maid.

SENEX. A maid.

ALL. A maid!
Everybody ought to have a maid.
Everybody ought to have a serving girl,
A loyal and unswerving girl
Who's quieter than a mouse.

Oh! Oh!
Think of her at the dustbin,
'Specially when she's just been
Traipsing about.
Oh! Oh!
Wouldn't she be delightful?

HYSTERIUM.
Living in . . .

SENEX.
Giving out . . .

ALL.
Everybody ought to have a maid,

Daintily collecting bits of paper 'n' strings,
Appealing in her apron strings,
Beguiling in her blouse!

HYSTERIUM.
Pattering through the attic,

SENEX.
Chattering in the cellar,

PSEUDOLUS.
Clattering in the kitchen,

SENEX.
Flattering in the bedroom,

ALL.
Puttering all around the house,
The house,
The house!

(LYCUS *enters.* HYSTERIUM *whispers to him.*)

LYCUS. A maid?

HYSTERIUM. A maid.

PSEUDOLUS. A maid.

SENEX. A maid!

ALL.
Everybody ought to have a maid,
Someone who's efficient and reliable,
Obedient and pliable
And quieter than a mouse.

Oh! Oh! Wouldn't she be so nimble,
Fiddling with her thimble,
Mending a gown?
Oh! Oh! Wouldn't she be delightful?

LYCUS.

Cleaning up . . .

SENEX.

Leaning down . . .

ALL.

Everybody ought to have a maid!
Someone who'll be busy as a bumblebee
And, even if you grumble, be
As graceful as a grouse!

LYCUS.

Wriggling in the anteroom,

HYSTERIUM.

Jiggling in the living-room,

PSEUDOLUS.

Giggling in the dining-room,

SENEX.

Wiggling in the other rooms,

ALL.

Puttering all around
The house!
The house!
The house!

(LYCUS *exits into his house.*)

SENEX. I know how busy both of you are. Therefore, it is for *me* to instruct her in the niceties of housework. (*Starting for his house.*) We shall start in my room.

HYSTERIUM. Sir!

PSEUDOLUS. Sir, your son is in there!

SENEX. Oh! (*Thinks a moment, then:*) Before my friend and neighbor, Erronius, went abroad in search of his children stolen in infancy by pirates, he asked me to look into his house from time to time. (*Goes to* ERRONIUS' *house, takes key from ledge and opens door.*) This seems as good a time as any. I shall have a chat with the girl in here. Send her to me.

PSEUDOLUS. Sir.

SENEX. Yes?

PSEUDOLUS. Only my great devotion to you allows me to speak so frankly. (*Unseen by* SENEX, PSEUDOLUS *sprinkles contents of vial on him.*) You trudged along the road quite some way, and I fear that the great physical exertion . . . (*Sniffs.*)

SENEX. (*Sniffing.*) Is that me?!

PSEUDOLUS. Yes, sir.

SENEX. My heavens, I smell like an overheated horse! I shall have to bathe.

PSEUDOLUS. At least!

(SENEX *exits into* ERRONIUS' *house.*)

HYSTERIUM. Why did I let her in the house? I should never have listened to you!

PSEUDOLUS. Everything is going to be fine, pussycat. (*Hands him potion book.*)

HYSTERIUM. Oh, you! You just see that she gets out of that house.

PSEUDOLUS. (*Picking up statue.*) And you just see that he *stays* in *that* house. Keep calm! (*Exits into* SENEX'S *house.*)

HYSTERIUM. Calm? Calm? Mustn't be excited. Calm. Calm. (*Sings excitedly.*)

I'm calm, I'm calm,
I'm perfectly calm,
I'm utterly under control.
I haven't a worry—
Where others would hurry,
I stroll.

(HE *runs frantically around the stage.*)

I'm calm, I'm cool,
A gibbering fool
Is something I never become!
When thunder is rumbling
And others are crumbling,
I hum.

(HE *tries to hum; it becomes a stifled scream.*)

I must think calm, comforting things:
Butterfly wings,
Emerald rings.
Or a murmuring brook,
Murmuring, murmuring, murmuring . . .
Look:

(*Steadying his hands, seemingly calm.*)

I'm calm, I'm calm,
I haven't a qualm,
I'm utterly under control.
Let nothing confuse me
Or faze me—
(*Yawns.*)
Excuse me—
I'm calm,
Oh, so calm,
Oh, so . . .

SENEX. (*Calls from inside* ERRONIUS' *house.*) Hysterium!

(HYSTERIUM *runs into* SENEX'S *house.* PROTEANS, *dressed as* SAILORS, *enter with bags, drop them, as* ERRONIUS *enters behind them.*)

ERRONIUS. Bring up the baggage. Fetch the rest from the harbor. (SAILORS *exit.*) Ah, home at last! After years of searching for my long lost children. (HYSTERIUM *enters from* SENEX'S *house, carrying plucked chicken, reacts in horror.*) How good it is to see this street once more. These tired old eyes fill with tears at the sight of the little they see. (*Bumps into* HYSTERIUM.) Pardon me, young woman, I was just . . . that is . . . I mean to say . . . Ah, lovely baby. (*Pats chicken.*) About the age of my children when they were stolen by pirates.—(*Going to his house.*) Well, at least I have the comfort of my lonely house.

(HYSTERIUM *rushes to door of* ERRONIUS' *house.*)

HYSTERIUM. Sir!

ERRONIUS. And who are you?

HYSTERIUM. Hysterium, sir, servant to Senex.

ERRONIUS. (*To pillar.*) Yes, of course. I should have known you anywhere. (SENEX *is heard singing from inside house a bit of "Everybody Ought To Have a Maid."*) What was that?

HYSTERIUM. I didn't hear anything.

(SENEX *sings a bit more.*)

HYSTERIUM. I didn't hear that either.

ERRONIUS. You did not hear that eerie sound?

HYSTERIUM. Eerie?

ERRONIUS. Eerie, as if haunted.

HYSTERIUM. (*To himself.*) Eerie, as if haunted? (*To* ER-
RONIUS.) Sir, what I am about to tell you is eerie. . . .
Your house is . . . is haunted.

ERRONIUS. Haunted?

HYSTERIUM. As haunted as the day is long!

(PSEUDOLUS *enters, stirring the potion, listens.*)

ERRONIUS. Impossible! My house haunted, you say? Strange.

HYSTERIUM. But true. Perhaps you ought to stay with relatives . . . distant relatives.

ERRONIUS. Yes! No! Fetch me a soothsayer.

HYSTERIUM. A soothsayer?

ERRONIUS. Yes, I must have him search my house immediately.

(PSEUDOLUS *puts cloth over his head, runs to* ERRONIUS,
chants ghoulishly.)

PSEUDOLUS. You are in need of a soothsayer?

ERRONIUS. How did you know?

PSEUDOLUS. I'd be a fine soothsayer if I didn't!

ERRONIUS. There is a spirit in my . . .

PSEUDOLUS. Silence! I am about to say the sooth! Wait!
(*Chants incoherently.*) I see it. I see everything. (HYS-
TERIUM *steps behind* ERRONIUS, *pantomimes distance.*)
You have been abroad.

ERRONIUS. Yes, yes.

PSEUDOLUS. For . . . (*Looks at* HYSTERIUM, *who flashes his
ten fingers twice.*) . . . twenty years! (ERRONIUS *nods
vigorously.* HYSTERIUM *shades his eyes with one hand.*)
You have been searching . . . for . . . (HYSTERIUM

60

cradles his arms, rocks them.) A child! (HYSTERIUM *holds up two fingers.*) Two children!

ERRONIUS. Yes, yes!

(HYSTERIUM *flexes his muscles.*)

PSEUDOLUS. A fine, big boy.

ERRONIUS. Yes.

PSEUDOLUS. And . . . (HYSTERIUM *places hand on his hip, pantomimes a girl.*) A strange, little boy. (HYSTERIUM *shakes his head "no."*) A girl! A girl! A boy and a girl!

ERRONIUS. Yes! Can you find them for me?

PSEUDOLUS. Certainly. I can find them for you.

ERRONIUS. (*Takes ring from his finger, gives it to* PSEUDOLUS.) Each wears a ring on which is engraven a gaggle of geese.

PSEUDOLUS. A gaggle of what?

ERRONIUS. A gaggle of geese. Look! (*Points to ring.*) There are only two others like it in the world. And my children wear them.

PSEUDOLUS. How many geese in a gaggle?

ERRONIUS. At least seven.

PSEUDOLUS. Seven? Then before I say the sooth again you must walk seven times around the seven hills of Rome.

ERRONIUS. Seven times?

HYSTERIUM. Slowly.

ERRONIUS. Seven times around the seven hills? (SAILORS *enter with more baggage.*) Take it all back to the harbor! (*Proudly.*) *My* house is haunted. (SAILORS *exit with bag-*

gage. SENEX *is heard singing again.* PSEUDOLUS *joins in, eerily.*) And the spirit?

PSEUDOLUS. It shall be gone by the time you have done my bidding.

ERRONIUS. Thank you.

PSEUDOLUS. To the hills!

ERRONIUS. To the hills! (*Starts for the footlights,* PSEUDOLUS *and* HYSTERIUM *stop him, head him toward the wings.*)

HYSTERIUM. This is the way, sir!

ERRONIUS. Thank you, young woman! (*Exits.*)

PSEUDOLUS. (*Calls.*) Sir, you forgot your gaggle! (*Puts ring on his own finger.* SENEX *enters from* ERRONIUS' *house.*)

SENEX. Hysterium!

HYSTERIUM. Sir!

SENEX. Prepare my bath!

HYSTERIUM. Yes, sir! (*Runs into* ERRONIUS' *house.*)

SENEX. Ah, Pseudolus, that little maid. Do you know what her first words were to me? She said "Take me."

PSEUDOLUS. (*Picking up potion bowl.*) And you shall, sir.

SENEX. . . . I'll try.

PSEUDOLUS. (*Exiting into* SENEX'S *house.*) Yes, sir.

SENEX. (*Starting into* ERRONIUS' *house.*) Remember, Hysterium. Not too hot and not too cold.

(HERO *runs on, calling.*)

HERO. Philia! Philia!

SENEX. Son!

HERO. Father! Where's Mother?

SENEX. (*Frightened, turns.*) Where?! (*Realizes.*) Oh. I—I have returned without her. Pressing business. (PHILIA *appears on balcony of* SENEX'S *house.*) Lovely new maid.

HERO. New maid?

SENEX. Pseudolus told me about it.

HERO. Oh.

SENEX. (*To* PHILIA.) Presently, my dear.

> (PHILIA *exits into house, waving.* SENEX *turns to audience, sings.*)

Why did he look at her that way?

HERO. (*Sings, to audience.*)
Why did he look at her that way?

BOTH.
Must be my imagination . . .

SENEX.
She's a lovely, blooming flower,
He's just a sprout—impossible!

HERO.
She's a lovely blooming flower,
He's all worn out—impossible!

SENEX.
Just a fledging in the nest . . .

HERO.
Just a man who needs a rest . . .

SENEX.
He's a beamish boy at best . . .

HERO.
Poor old fellow . . .

SENEX.
He's a child and love's a test
He's too young to pass—impassable!

HERO.
He has asthma, gout, a wife,
Lumbago and gas—irascible!

SENEX.
Romping in the nursery . . .

HERO.
He looks tired . . .

SENEX. (*To* HERO, *warmly.*)
Son, sit on your father's knee.

HERO. (*To* SENEX, *warmly.*)
Father, you can lean on me.

BOTH. (*To audience.*)
Him?
Impossible!

HERO.
But why did she wave at him that way?

SENEX.
Why did she wave at him that way?

BOTH.
Could there be an explanation?

HERO.
Women often want a father,
She may want mine—it's possible!

SENEX.
He's a handsome lad of twenty,
I'm thirty-nine—it's possible!

HERO.
Older men know so much more . . .

SENEX.
In a way, I'm forty-four . . .

HERO.
Next to him, I'll seem a bore . . .

SENEX.
All right, fifty!

HERO.
Then again, he *is* my father,
I ought to trust—impossible!

SENEX.
Then again, with love at my age,
Sometimes it's just—impossible!

HERO.
With a girl, I'm ill-at-ease . . .

SENEX.
I don't feel well . . .

HERO. (*To* SENEX, *helplessly.*)
Sir, about those birds and bees . . .

SENEX. (*To* HERO, *helplessly.*)
Son, a glass of water, please . . .

BOTH. (*To audience.*)
The situation's fraught,
Fraughter than I thought,
With horrible,

65

Impossible
Possibilities!

SENEX. (*Calling to his house.*) Pseudolus! (*To* HERO.) Son, it grieves me to see a boy your age moping about the house. (PSEUDOLUS *enters, stirring potion.*) Pseudolus, I want you to take Hero to the baths.

HERO. Sir!

PSEUDOLUS. Very good, sir. Allow me to finish a brew master Hero asked me to prepare. (*To* HERO.) Master, I shall meet you in front of the baths of Aqua Salina. You know where it is? Next to the harbor. And I shall have a surprise for you.

HERO. Oh, yes. Yes, of course. Farewell, father. Farewell, Pseudolus. (*Exits.*)

SENEX. Well, he to his bath and I to mine.

(HYSTERIUM *enters from* ERRONIUS' *house, wiping hands on tunic.*)

HYSTERIUM. Just the way you like it, sir.

SENEX. One thing more, Hysterium.

HYSTERIUM. Yes, sir?

SENEX. I shall need a complete change of garb. Let me see . . . my tunic with the tassels!

HYSTERIUM. Sir, it needs taking in.

SENEX. Well, take it in and bring it out! (*Exits into* ERRONIUS' *house.*)

(HYSTERIUM *exits into* SENEX'S *house singing a bit of "I'm Calm."* LYCUS *enters from his house.*)

LYCUS. Pseudolus! The girl! I want to know the worst. How is she?

PSEUDOLUS. She is very low.

LYCUS. Still smiling?

PSEUDOLUS. Laughing! (LYCUS *reacts in horror.*) There is one hope! I have prepared a plague potion. If it is not too late, we may yet save her life.

LYCUS. Give it to her!

PSEUDOLUS. Yes!

> (PSEUDOLUS *starts for* SENEX'S *house as* FANFARE *is heard and* PROTEAN, *dressed as* SOLDIER, *enters, carrying spear.*)

SOLDIER. Ho, there! (THEY *turn, stare at him with horror.*) I seek the house of Marcus Lycus.

LYCUS. (*Stammering superbly.*) Who heeks the souse of Mycus Leecus?

PSEUDOLUS. (*A hand on* LYCUS' *shoulder.*) Hold, sir.

LYCUS. But he . . . who . . .

PSEUDOLUS. You're not holding. (*To* SOLDIER, *enunciating grotesquely.*) Who is he who seeks the house of Marcus Lycus?

SOLDIER. A foot soldier of Captain Miles Gloriosus! (*Executes an elaborate salute.*)

PSEUDOLUS. Smartly done!

SOLDIER. My captain has dispatched me to inform you that he is but half a league away. Prepare to greet him! (*Salutes, exits.*)

PSEUDOLUS. Half a league!

LYCUS. We have only moments!

PSEUDOLUS. I'll give her the potion!

LYCUS. Yes!

PSEUDOLUS. Yes! (*Starts for* SENEX'S *house.*)

LYCUS. Wait!

PSEUDOLUS. (*Returns to* LYCUS.) What?

LYCUS. Don't leave me!

PSEUDOLUS. Why not?

LYCUS. He's coming!

PSEUDOLUS. I know he's coming!

LYCUS. (*Takes bowl from him.*) You speak to him. *I'll* give her the potion!

PSEUDOLUS. Wait! You can't give her the potion!

LYCUS. Why not?

PSEUDOLUS. You'll catch the plague!

LYCUS. (*Hands him bowl quickly.*) Oh, I don't want the plague!

PSEUDOLUS. I've got to give her the potion!

LYCUS. Yes!

PSEUDOLUS. Yes! (*Starts for* SENEX'S *house.*)

LYCUS. Wait!

PSEUDOLUS. What? (*Returns to* LYCUS.)

LYCUS. She is in the house of Senex!

PSEUDOLUS. What will we do? . . . Does he know which house is your house?

LYCUS. No!

PSEUDOLUS. (*Points to* SENEX'S *house.*) *This* is your house!

LYCUS. Will he believe it?

PSEUDOLUS. Get the girls!

LYCUS. Good!

PSEUDOLUS. I'll give her the potion!

LYCUS. And I'll get the girls!

PSEUDOLUS. Good!

LYCUS. Yes!

PSEUDOLUS. Yes! (*Starts for* SENEX'S *house.*)

LYCUS. Wait!

PSEUDOLUS. (*Returns to* LYCUS.) *What is it??!!*

LYCUS. I forgot.

PSEUDOLUS. Lycus, we must not lose our heads!

LYCUS. Yes! No!

PSEUDOLUS. (*Screams.*) We must remain serene!

(FANFARE *is heard.*)

LYCUS. Pseudolus, *you* speak to the captain! I have no talent for bravery.

PSEUDOLUS. You grant me permission to represent you?

LYCUS. Complete!

PSEUDOLUS. All right. Collect the courtesans and bring them out. Then you are to wait in your house.

LYCUS. Pseudolus, I am eternally grateful! I am your friend until death!

PSEUDOLUS. Go!

LYCUS. Yes!

PSEUDOLUS. Yes! (*Starts for* SENEX'S *house.*)

LYCUS. Wait!

PSEUDOLUS. (*Stops, yells.*) No!

(*A* FANFARE, *and* TWO PROTEANS, *dressed as* SOLDIERS, *enter, come to a smart halt.* LYCUS *ducks into his house.* PSEUDOLUS *puts down potion bowl.*)

SECOND SOLDIER. Ho, there!

THIRD SOLDIER. We seek the house of Marcus Lycus!

PSEUDOLUS. Who seeks the mouse of Larus Heekus?

THIRD SOLDIER. Foot soldiers of Captain Miles Gloriosus.

SECOND SOLDIER. He is but a quarter of a league away and bids you honor this. (*Hands* PSEUDOLUS *parchment.*)

PSEUDOLUS. (*Studies parchment.*) Oh, yes, of course.

SECOND SOLDIER. You know what this is?

PSEUDOLUS. Of course I know what this is. This is writing.

THIRD SOLDIER. It is your contract with the captain.

PSEUDOLUS. And a pretty piece of work. What is this word here? (*Points to spot on parchment.*)

THIRD SOLDIER. That is "Lycus."

PSEUDOLUS. Oh, yes. Then you realize whom you are speaking to.

SECOND SOLDIER. Yes, sir.

THIRD SOLDIER. And do you see what it says there? (*Points to another spot.*)

PSEUDOLUS. It says . . . words. And I intend to stand behind those words, or my name is not Marcus Lycus!

(HYSTERIUM *enters.*)

70

HYSTERIUM. Pseudolus!

PSEUDOLUS. (*Without missing a beat.*) Or my name is not Pseudolus Marcus Lycus! A moment. I must have a word with my eunuch. (*Taking* HYSTERIUM *aside.*) Come here, eunuch!

HYSTERIUM. How dare you call me that?

PSEUDOLUS. You know it's not true, and I know it's not true, so what do we care what they think?

HYSTERIUM. Those soldiers, have they come for the girl? I'll go right in and get her.

PSEUDOLUS. They have not come for the girl. They have come for me.

HYSTERIUM. What?

PSEUDOLUS. Hysterium, I have never told you this, but years ago I deserted from the army.

HYSTERIUM. No!

PSEUDOLUS. Sh! I was very young. I wanted to be an archer. Instead, they made me a slinger. Then, one day, at the height of battle, I lost my head. I arched when I should have slung. I had to flee.

HYSTERIUM. And now they have found you. Oh, Pseudolus!

PSEUDOLUS. Sh! They are looking for Pseudolus. I told them I am Lycus.

HYSTERIUM. And Lycus you are! Rely on me!

PSEUDOLUS. I must. (*Picks up potion bowl.*) Hysterium, more bad news!

HYSTERIUM. I hope it's good.

PSEUDOLUS. It's terrible! The girl refuses to go with her captain. That is why I have prepared your sleeping potion. You

71

are to give her a drop or two in a beaker of wine, and upon hearing me say "Present the bride," carry her out in your arms!

HYSTERIUM. Trust me, Pseu—(*Catches himself, then loudly.*) Trust me, Lycus! (*Takes bowl from* PSEUDOLUS, *speaking for* SOLDIERS' *benefit.*) I go, Lycus. Farewell, Lycus! (*Exits into* SENEX'S *house.*)

PSEUDOLUS. (*To* SOLDIERS.) Bid your captain come! His bride awaits him! (SOLDIERS *execute fancy salute, run off.* PSEUDOLUS *calls out.*) Lycus! The girls! Quickly!

LYCUS. (*Opening his door.*) Yes! Eunuchs! The girls! Quickly! (*To* PSEUDOLUS.) We shall pose them informally!

PSEUDOLUS. Give the place a friendly look.

(EUNUCHS *herd* COURTESANS *out of house.*)

EUNUCH. Hurry, there! Hurry! Hurry!

GYMNASIA. Don't you lower your voice to me!

LYCUS. You are to do exactly as Pseudolus bids. He will represent me.

PSEUDOLUS. (*Points to* SENEX'S *house.*) All you girls over here! Now, you eunuchs . . . (*Indicates manly pose* HE *wants them to assume.* EUNUCHS *squeal with delight.*) Lycus, do we really need these eunuchs?

LYCUS. (*To* EUNUCHS.) Into the house.

EUNUCHS. (*Chirping.*) Into the house! Into the house! (EUNUCHS *exit into* LYCUS' *house.* PSEUDOLUS *arranges courtesans.*)

PSEUDOLUS. (*To* PANACEA.) You there. (*To* TINTINABULA *and* VIBRATA.) You there. (*To* GEMINAE.) You there. (*To* GYMNASIA.) You there . . . Oh, there's so much of you there! (*Leans on her bosom, as* ERRONIUS *enters.*)

72

ERRONIUS. First time around! (ALL *watch as* HE *crosses stage, exits.*)

PSEUDOLUS. (*To* COURTESANS.) May I have your attention? You are about to meet a great captain. Remember who you are and what you stand for. Now, will you all please strike . . . vocational attitudes? (COURTESANS *strike poses.*) Perfect! I would like a mosaic of this scene. An entire wall made up of . . .

(FANFARE *is heard.*)

LYCUS. The Captain! Pseudolus, again my heartfelt . . .

PSEUDOLUS. In! In!

(LYCUS *exits into his house. A* SECOND FANFARE *is heard.*)

MILES' VOICE. (*Offstage.*) Stand aside, everyone! I take large steps! (*Enters with* SOLDIERS, *counting off.*)

SOLDIERS.
One, two, one, two . . .

MILES.
We not only fought but we won, too!

SOLDIERS.
One, two, one, two . . .
Left, right, left, right . . .

MILES.
There's none of the enemy left, right?

SOLDIERS.
Right! Left! . . . uh . . . Ri—uh—left!

(*Utter confusion.*)

MILES. Halt!

PSEUDOLUS. (*Saluting.*) Hail, Miles Gloriosus!

73

MILES. You are?

PSEUDOLUS. Marcus Lycus, sir. I am dazzled by your presence.

MILES. Everyone is.

PSEUDOLUS. (*Indicating* SENEX's *house.*) Welcome to my house, great captain. Your bride awaits you.

MILES. My bride! (*Sings.*)
My bride! My bride!
I've come to claim my bride,
Come tenderly to crush her against my side!
Let haste be made,
I cannot be delayed!
There are lands to conquer,
Cities to loot,
And peoples to degrade!

SOLDIERS.
Look at those arms!
Look at that chest!
Look at them!

MILES.
Not to mention the rest!
Even I am impressed.

My bride! My bride!
Come bring to me my bride!
My lust for her no longer can be denied!
Convey the news,
I have no time to lose!
There are towns to plunder,
Temples to burn
And women to abuse!

SOLDIERS.
Look at that foot!

74

Look at that heel!
Mark the magnificent muscles of steel!

MILES.

I am my ideal!

I, Miles Gloriosus,
I, slaughterer of thousands,
I, oppressor of the meek,
Subduer of the weak,
Degrader of the Greek,
Destroyer of the Turk,
Must hurry back to work!

MILES.	COURTESANS.	SOLDIERS.
I, Miles Gloriosus,	Him, Miles Gloriosus,	A man among men!
I, paragon of virtues,	Him, paragon of virtues,	With sword and with pen!

MILES.		ALL.
I, in war the most admired,		Himmm!
In wit the most inspired,		Himmmm!
In love the most desired,		Himmm!
In dress the best displayed,		
I am a parade!		

SOLDIERS.

Look at those eyes,
Cunning and keen!
Look at the size of those thighs,
Like a mighty machine!

PSEUDOLUS.

Those are the mightiest thighs that I ever have theen!
I mean . . .

MILES.

My bride! My bride!
Inform my lucky bride:

The fabled arms of Miles are open wide!
Make haste! Make haste!
I have no time to waste!
There are shrines I should be sacking,
Ribs I should be cracking,
Eyes to gouge and booty to divide!
Bring me my bride!

SOLDIERS.
Bring him his bride!

ALL.
Bring him his bride!

(PSEUDOLUS *goes to* SENEX'S *house.*)

PSEUDOLUS. Present the bride! (FANFARE.) Pay homage all!
Here, in one being is Juno, Diana and Venus. (ALL *kneel.*)
Present the bride! (FANFARE. PSEUDOLUS *bows.* HYSTERIUM
enters.) (*To* MILES.) A short delay, sir! (*Pulls* HYSTERIUM
aside.) What happened?

HYSTERIUM. I'll tell you what happened? Nothing! She won't
drink!

PSEUDOLUS. What?

HYSTERIUM. She says on Crete her religion forbids it.

PSEUDOLUS. He had to fall in love with a religious Cretan!
I'll get her to drink! Captain, forgive the girl. She primps
and preens. She wants to be worthy of so great a warrior.

(*Exits into* SENEX'S *house with* HYSTERIUM.)

MILES. Understandable. I *am* a legend in my own time.
(*Laughs.* SOLDIERS *join in.*) Men! Close ranks! Stand tall!
Lycus! (PSEUDOLUS *re-enters as* LYCUS *peeks out of upper
window of his house, listens.*) Where is my bride?

PSEUDOLUS. Did she not come through this door?

MILES. No! What are you saying, man?

PSEUDOLUS. The virgin has escaped!

MILES. Oh, no! The beautiful bride I bargained for!

PSEUDOLUS. Vanished!

MILES. This is monstrous!

PSEUDOLUS. It certainly is. But look at it this way. Since I cannot deliver her to you, you do not have to pay me the 500 minae.

MILES. I *paid* you the 500 minae! (PSEUDOLUS *reacts*.) Through my agents. Has the money escaped as well?

PSEUDOLUS. There has been a little mistake. (*Laughs weakly*.) I was only joking. Lycus will pay you.

(LYCUS *groans, disappears from window*.)

MILES. What?

PSEUDOLUS. I was helping out a friend. Allow me, great captain. (HE *goes to* LYCUS' *house, pulls* LYCUS *out*.) Come out here! (*To* MILES.) Here is your man! (*To* LYCUS.) Tell him! Tell him who I am!

(HYSTERIUM *enters*.)

LYCUS. Everyone knows who you are, *Lycus*.

HYSTERIUM. Of course. He is Marcus Lycus.

PSEUDOLUS. No! No! *He* is Lycus. *This* is his house!

LYCUS. (*To* MILES.) Look within, sir. You will find none here but hooded men. We are a holy order. An ancient brotherhood of lepers. (MILES *backs away*.) Unclean! Unclean! And bless you, Lycus! (HE *backs offstage*.)

MILES. What now, Lycus?

PSEUDOLUS. What?

MILES. I shall tell you what! With axe and pike, my soldiers shall raze this house to the ground!

HYSTERIUM. (*Fainting.*) Our beautiful house!

MILES. And you, you shall receive the maximum punishment, death!

(COURTESANS *scream.*)

PSEUDOLUS. Please, sir, please! May I be allowed a word?

MILES. A word?

PSEUDOLUS. One word.

MILES. It had better be a good one.

PSEUDOLUS. Oh, it is, sir!

MILES. What is it?

PSEUDOLUS. (*To audience.*) Intermission!

END OF ACT I

ACT TWO

❦ ❦ ❦

PROLOGUS. Welcome again, playgoers. You are about to wit-
ness the second half of our play. (*Signals orchestra, which
plays under following.*) Permit me to remind you where we
were when last you saw us. The virgin . . . (PHILIA *enters.*) . . . was waiting . . . that's what they do best
. . . waiting here in the house for her captain to claim
her. She has refused to drink the potion on religious grounds.
(PHILIA *exits into* SENEX's *house.*) Lycus . . . (LYCUS *enters.*) . . . skulks about the city, searching for Philia.
(LYCUS *exits.*) Hero . . . (HERO *enters.*) . . . is at the
baths where he sits and soaks. (HERO *exits.*) His mother
. . . (DOMINA *enters, exits.*) . . . is on the way to the
country to visit *her* mother. A hundred and four years old,
and not one organ in working condition. The courtesans
. . . (COURTESANS *enter.*) . . . Miles Gloriosus and his
mighty warriors . . . (MILES, SOLDIERS *enter.*) . . . Hysterium and Pseudolus are here. (HYSTERIUM, PSEUDOLUS
enter.) And I, Senex, await the maid in my neighbor's
house, hopefully about to sow my last oat, if memory serves.
Let the play continue! (*Exits into* ERRONIUS' *house.*)

PSEUDOLUS. (*To* MILES.) Sir! I . . .

MILES. (*To* SOLDIERS.) Gag him! (SOLDIER *grabs* PSEUDOLUS
from behind, clamps hand over his mouth.) And now I rid

79

Rome of a rascal! (HE *is about to send his sword into* PSEUDOLUS, *who whirls around. The sword jabs* SOLDIER *in the rear.* SOLDIER *jumps away, rubbing sore spot.* MILES *advances on* PSEUDOLUS.) You . . .

PSEUDOLUS. Sir! (MILES *stalks him.*) The girl must be near at hand. If you kill me you deprive yourself of seeing a face so fair, a heart so pure, a body so undulating . . . (MILES *lowers his sword.* PSEUDOLUS, *sensing success, presses on.*) She is magnificence personified! If you had been born a woman, you would have been she!

MILES. As magnificent as that?

PSEUDOLUS. Yes, sir. Spare me! I am sure she can be found.

MILES. You are?

PSEUDOLUS. Yes, sir. I shall give you a list of ten or twenty places you might look for her.

MILES. *You* shall look for her!

PSEUDOLUS. Me? With this bad leg? (*Limps horribly.*)

MILES. With that bad leg!

PSEUDOLUS. Yes, it will do it good. And where may I deliver the girl? I mean, where will you be?

MILES. (*Points to* SENEX's *house.*) Waiting here in your house.

HYSTERIUM. No!

MILES. No?!

HYSTERIUM. I meant "yes," it just came out "no."

MILES. (*To* PSEUDOLUS.) And to assure your return . . . Men! You are to go with him.

PSEUDOLUS. Sir, before I go, a word with my eunuch.

MILES. Be brief.

PSEUDOLUS. Yes, sir. Come here, eunuch. (*Pulls* HYSTERIUM *aside.*) Hysterium, this is what you must do. Hide the girl, up on the roof.

HYSTERIUM. Why?

PSEUDOLUS. Why not? Go.

(HYSTERIUM *exits into* SENEX'S *house.*)

PSEUDOLUS. My eunuch is making sure the house is fit to receive so illustrious a visitor.

MILES. I have been put off enough for one day! (*Turns to enter house, stops, as* ERRONIUS *enters.*)

ERRONIUS. The second time around! (*Exits.*)

MILES. Lycus!

PSEUDOLUS. Yes, sir! (*Calls.*) Ready?

HYSTERIUM. (*From inside* SENEX'S *house.*) Ready!

PSEUDOLUS. All is ready, sir. There is food and drink within. And the girls will sing and dance for you.

(COURTESANS *exit into* SENEX'S *house.*)

MILES. You have but one hour. Men, you are to hound his every step. (*Exits into* SENEX'S *house.* PSEUDOLUS *circles stage, followed by* SOLDIERS, THEY *exit.* SENEX *appears in window of* ERRONIUS' *house.*)

SENEX. Hysterium!

(HYSTERIUM *re-enters.*)

HYSTERIUM. Yes, sir!

SENEX. Tell the little maid I am almost ready.

HYSTERIUM. Sir, I must say this to you. Abandon this mad adventure! Think of your wife on the way to the country!

81

SENEX. *That,* Hysterium, is the country's problem.

HYSTERIUM. Yes, sir.

SENEX. Hysterium, one thing more. You know that potion you prepare that so fills one with passion, one can almost perform miracles?

HYSTERIUM. Yes, sir. We have some left over from your last anniversary.

SENEX. Bring it to me now, slave-in-chief. (*Exits into house.*)

HYSTERIUM. Slave-in-chief! I wonder how many slaves-in-chief have a master in the tub, a house full of courtesans, and a virgin on the roof! (*Exits into* SENEX'S *house, as* PSEUDO- LUS *enters, closely followed by* SOLDIERS. HE *does several intricate maneuvers which the* SOLDIERS *carefully follow. The maneuvers become more elaborate.* PANACEA *enters from* SENEX'S *house, and* SOLDIERS *follow her off.*)

PSEUDOLUS. (*To audience.*) Just one hour. Pretending she was dead was the perfect plan. If only Philia had taken one sip . . . It still is the perfect plan, if I can only find a body. A body. (*An inspiration.*) Gusto! Gusto, the bodysnatcher! He owes me a favor! (HE *runs off, not seeing* DOMINA, *who enters, addresses audience.*)

DOMINA. Since sending my husband back to Rome, I have been haunted by the premonition that he is up to something low. (*Calls.*) Hysterium!

HYSTERIUM. (*Entering from* SENEX'S *house with cup.*) Coming master . . . mistress! You're home!

DOMINA. And parched with thirst, ever-thoughtful Hysterium. (*Reaches for cup,* HE *pulls it away.*)

HYSTERIUM. No! It's a potion!

DOMINA. What sort of potion?

HYSTERIUM. To make you thirsty. And you're already thirsty, so you don't need it. (*Puts cup near* ERRONIUS' *house.*)

DOMINA. Thirst is the lesser of my problems. Hysterium, on the best of intuition, I believe my husband is fouling the nest.

HYSTERIUM. No! Never!

DOMINA. Never? Old friend and confidant, you are talking to a woman who faces facts. (*Sings.*)
For over thirty years,
I've cried myself to sleep,
Assailed by doubts and fears
So great the gods themselves would weep!
The moment I am gone,
I wonder where he'll go.
In all your simple honesty,
You can't begin to know . . .
Ohhhh . . .

(*Wailing tenderly.*)

I want him,
I need him,
Where is he?

(*Furiously.*)

That dirty old man is here somewhere,
Cavorting with someone young and fair,
Disporting in every shameless whim,
Just wait till I get my hands on him!

(*Tenderly.*)

I'll hold him,
Enfold him,
Where is he?

(*Furiously.*)

83

That dirty old man, where can he be?
Profaning our vows for all to see,
Complaining how he's misunderstood,
Abusing me (if he only would!)
Oh, love,
Sweet love,
Why hide?
You vermin, you worm, you villain!
Come face,
Embrace
Your bride!
Wherever he is, I know he's still an
Angel,
My angel!
Where is he,
That dirty old man divine?
I love him,
I love him,
That lecherous, lewd, lascivious,
Loathsome, lying, lazy,
Dirty old man of mine!

MILES' VOICE. (*From inside* SENEX'S *house.*) Why?

DOMINA. Ah, I hear him now!

MILES. Why must I always be surrounded by fawning admirers?

DOMINA. That is not my husband's voice. Tell me, who is in my house?

HYSTERIUM. I think it's a captain.

DOMINA. A captain?

HYSTERIUM. Yes . . . he thinks that . . . your house . . . is the . . . I hope you do not object to my offering him your hospitality.

DOMINA. Object? When, I, myself, am the daughter of a Roman general? Hysterium, I must meet him.

HYSTERIUM. You wouldn't like him. He's very vulgar.

DOMINA. All soldiers are, in a grand sort of way.

(MILES *appears in doorway.*)

MILES. . . . interminable! (*Shouts at* HYSTERIUM.) Bring more food and drink, eunuch!

HYSTERIUM. (*To* DOMINA.) You see?

DOMINA. Captain, I was just coming inside to give you a proper welcome.

(HYSTERIUM *winces.*)

MILES. (*Points to* SENEX'S *house.*) You are of this house?

DOMINA. For years and years. You know, Captain, my father was General Magnus. On the last anniversary of his death, I entertained over two hundred officers.

MILES. Two hundred? By yourself?

DOMINA. Of course not. Hysterium here was a big help. (HYS-TERIUM *smiles proudly, then reacts painfully.*) But now my business takes me to the Forum, but I shall return. And for the length of your stay I shall bend over backwards to please you.

MILES. (*Horrified.*) That will not be necessary! (*Exits into* SENEX'S *house.*)

DOMINA. I do wish I could chat on with him, but I must find out why my husband was so anxious to return to Rome. Hysterium, when next we meet I shall be in some form of disguise. If you recognize me, not a word. (*Waving to* MILES, *who appears in door of house.*) Until later, captain. (MILES *moans, exits into house.* DOMINA *starts off, as* PSEU-

DOLUS *enters, sees her, starts polishing pillar.*) Ah, Pseudolus, busy as ever.

PSEUDOLUS. Yes, madam. (SHE *exits.* PSEUDOLUS *rushes to* HYSTERIUM.) She's back!

HYSTERIUM. Yes!

PSEUDOLUS. What has happened?

HYSTERIUM. What *hasn't* happened?

PSEUDOLUS. All right, what *hasn't* happened? She hasn't found out anything, has she?

HYSTERIUM. No!

PSEUDOLUS. Good!

HYSTERIUM. But she will, and she'll kill me!

PSEUDOLUS. No, she won't!

HYSTERIUM. No, she won't. I'll kill myself! I can do it painlessly. If she does it, it will hurt. I must do it. I have besmirched the honor of my family. My father will turn in his grave!

PSEUDOLUS. Your father is alive.

HYSTERIUM. This will kill him!

PSEUDOLUS. Are you finished? Now, listen to this. I have really shocking news.

HYSTERIUM. What?

PSEUDOLUS. You know Gusto, the bodysnatcher? He died this morning.

HYSTERIUM. No! I saw him only yesterday. When is he to be buried?

PSEUDOLUS. They don't know. Someone snatched the body.

HYSTERIUM. Isn't that a sha—? (*Does a take.*) Why are we crying over a dead bodysnatcher?!

PSEUDOLUS. Because he could have helped us. He could have lent us a body. (*Puts his hand on* HYSTERIUM'S *shoulder.*)

HYSTERIUM. A body?

PSEUDOLUS. A body. (*A gleam comes into his eye, starts running his hand over* HYSTERIUM'S *shoulder and chest.*) A body. Hysterium, would you like everything to be the way it was when you woke up this morning?

HYSTERIUM. In a minute!

PSEUDOLUS. That's all it will take. Come! (*Pulls* HYSTERIUM *to* LYCUS' *house.*)

HYSTERIUM. In here?

PSEUDOLUS. In here!

HYSTERIUM. Where did you get the money? (PSEUDOLUS *pulls* HYSTERIUM *into* LYCUS' *house.*)

(SENEX *enters from* ERRONIUS' *house, inhales deeply.*)

SENEX. Mmmmmmm. (*To audience.*) Something smells divine, and it's me. I just took the most luxurious bath. The oil, the essences. Oh, spectators, I would love to pass among you so that each and every one might get a good whiff. (*Calls.*) Philia! (*To himself.*) Mustn't shout. I have to save every bit of energy. (*Gently.*) Philia.

(PHILIA *appears on roof of* SENEX'S *house.*)

PHILIA. Yes, master? Master?

SENEX. (*Looks around for her, then sees her on roof.*) Ah, my dear. No need to dust up there. Come to me.

PHILIA. I am yours.

SENEX. Yes, my dear. But not on the roof. Join me in this house.

PHILIA. Yes, sir.

(SENEX *exits into* ERRONIUS' *house. As* PHILIA *disappears from roof,* MILES *appears on balcony of* SENEX'S *house.*)

MILES. Oh, where is he? If he does not bring me my bride he shall see me at the height of my wrath. (*Looks down, gets dizzy, emits a tiny scream, and staggers back into house.*)

(PHILIA *enters from* SENEX'S *house, as* HERO *runs on.*)

HERO. Philia!

PHILIA. In time to say farewell.

HERO. Did not Pseudolus give you a beaker of wine?

PHILIA. My religion forbids the drinking of wine.

HERO. Oh, no!

PHILIA. Oh, yes.

HERO. Oh, Philia.

PHILIA. The captain. I must go to him.

HERO. I hate him.

PHILIA. So do I. And I have a way to make him suffer. (*Sings.*)
Let the captain wed me and woo me,
I shall play my part!
Let him make his mad passion to me,
You will have my heart!
He can have the body he paid for,
Nothing but the body he paid for!
When he has the body he paid for,
Our revenge will start!

When I kiss him,
I'll be kissing you,

88

So I'll kiss him morning and night,
That'll show him!

When I hold him,
I'll be holding you,
So I'll hold him ten times as tight,
That'll show him, too!

I shall coo and tenderly stroke his hair.
Wish that you were there—
You'd enjoy it!

When it's evening
And we're in our tent for two,
I'll sit on his knee,
Get to know him
Intimately,
That'll show him
How much I really love you!

> (PSEUDOLUS *enters from* LYCUS' *house.*)

HERO. Pseudolus!

PSEUDOLUS. What has happened? Why are you not on the . . . ?

HERO. Her captain has come!

PSEUDOLUS. Where is he?

PHILIA. (*Points to* ERRONIUS' *house.*) In there.

PSEUDOLUS. In there . . . ? (*Realizes* SHE *is referring to* SENEX.) No, no, he *was* in there. He had to go to the Senate for an unexpected ovation.

HERO. Really?

PSEUDOLUS. (*Shaking his head "no."*) Of course.

PHILIA. Does he still want me to wait on the roof?

PSEUDOLUS. Yes.

MILES' VOICE. (*From inside* SENEX'S *house.*) Leave me alone!

PSEUDOLUS. No! Wait—uh—in the garden!

PHILIA. In the garden?

PSEUDOLUS. Yes. Behind that large clump of myrrh!

PHILIA. You will tell me when he comes?

PSEUDOLUS. Don't we always?

PHILIA. Oh, Hero, if only you could buy me from the captain.

PSEUDOLUS. If Hero has the captain's contract, you will go with him? (PHILIA *nods "yes."*) It shall be arranged. Into the garden. (HERO *and* PHILIA *exit into garden.* PSEUDOLUS *hums "Free" as* HE *pushes bench center stage.* HE *calls.*) Come out here! Come on out!

(HYSTERIUM *enters from* LYCUS' *house in virginal gown and wig.*)

HYSTERIUM. You didn't tell me I'd have to be a girl!

PSEUDOLUS. A dead girl! The captain will see you, go on his way, and all will be well.

HYSTERIUM. No! It won't do! (HE *starts back into house.* PSEUDOLUS *stops him.*)

PSEUDOLUS. Please, Hysterium. We must convince the captain.

HYSTERIUM. That I am a beautiful dead girl?

PSEUDOLUS. Yes.

HYSTERIUM. He'll never believe it.

PSEUDOLUS. He will. You're delicious.

HYSTERIUM. What if he tries to kiss me?

PSEUDOLUS. He won't kiss you.

HYSTERIUM. How can he help it if I'm so delicious?

PSEUDOLUS. Hysterium, please—just lie on the bench.

HYSTERIUM. He'll never believe I'm a girl. Look at me. Just look at me.

PSEUDOLUS. I can't take my eyes off you. (*Sings.*)
You're lovely,
Absolutely lovely,
Who'd believe the loveliness of you?

HYSTERIUM. No!

PSEUDOLUS. Come back! (*Sings.*)
Perfect,
Sweet and warm and winsome,
Radiant as in some dream come true.
Now
Venus will seem tame,
Helen and her thousand ships
Will have to die of shame!

(HYSTERIUM *is becoming convinced;* PSEUDOLUS *presses his advantage.*)

You're so lovely,
Frighteningly lovely,
That the world will never seem the same!

(*Gently forces* HYSTERIUM *to lie back on the bench, folds his arms. Speaks.*) Now, lie there, close your eyes, and think dead thoughts. Good! (*Starts into* SENEX'S *house, stops, with disgust, as* HYSTERIUM *sits up and sings.*)

HYSTERIUM.
I'm lovely,
Absolutely lovely,
Who'd believe the loveliness of me?

Perfect,
Sweet and warm and winsome,
Radiant as in some dream come true.

(PSEUDOLUS *forces him down on bench.*)

Now . . .

(*Speaks.*) Shouldn't I have jewelry?

PSEUDOLUS. Jewelry? (*Thinks a moment, takes* ERRONIUS'
ring from his finger, slips it on HYSTERIUM.)

HYSTERIUM. Flowers.

PSEUDOLUS. What?

HYSTERIUM. I should have flowers. (PSEUDOLUS *gives flower
to* HYSTERIUM. *Sings.*)
I'm so lovely,

PSEUDOLUS.
Literally lovely—

BOTH.
That the world will never seem the same—

PSEUDOLUS.
You look lovely—

BOTH.
That the world will never seem the same!

(PSEUDOLUS *gets him down on bench once more, covers
his face with the veil, and folds his arms.*)

PSEUDOLUS. Fold the arms!

HYSTERIUM. (*Sitting up.*) Any coins he puts in my eyes, I
keep! (PSEUDOLUS *pushes* HYSTERIUM *down.*)

FIRST SOLDIER'S VOICE. (*Offstage.*) Ho, there! (SOLDIERS *run
on in pursuit of* PANACEA, *who exits into* SENEX'S *house.*
PSEUDOLUS *stops* SOLDIERS.)

PSEUDOLUS. I have been looking everywhere for you. Here is your captain's bride. Dead! (SOLDIERS *crowd around* HYSTERIUM.) Give her air! (THEY *jump back.*) You had best break the sad news to your captain. (SOLDIER *enters* SENEX'S *house fearfully.* PSEUDOLUS *looks at* HYSTERIUM, *then to* SOLDIERS.) A virgin. A lot of good it did her. (MILES *enters with* SOLDIER.)

MILES. Oh, grievous day. Men, support me! (SOLDIERS *hold him.*) How? How did she die?

PSEUDOLUS. Well, she just sort of rolled over and . . .

MILES. Spare me! I cannot control my tears. I must cry.

PSEUDOLUS. Go ahead, you'll feel better. Now that you have seen her, sir, I suggest you depart and torture yourself no longer. If you'll give me the contract, I—I shall dispose of the body.

MILES. Ghoul! I will not leave without the comfort of a proper funeral service! (HYSTERIUM *shakes his head "no."* PSEUDOLUS *blocks* MILES' *view.*)

PSEUDOLUS. Sir, do you have time for that? I mean, isn't there a war somewhere you should be—

MILES. Silence! I insist on conducting a funeral.

PSEUDOLUS. Yes, sir.

MILES. We need mourners.

PSEUDOLUS. We have them. (*To* SOLDIERS.) Hold him firmly. (SOLDIERS *hold* MILES. PSEUDOLUS *exits into* SENEX'S *house.*)

MILES. The poor girl. To have died so young, without ever having experienced . . . me.

(PSEUDOLUS *re-enters.*)

93

PSEUDOLUS. Sir, they will be here presently. While we wait, would you like something to eat?

MILES. No, thank you. (*Wails.*) Oh, her bridal bower becomes a burial bier of bitter bereavement.

PSEUDOLUS. Very good. Can you say, "Titus, the tailor, told ten tall tales to Titania, the titmouse?"

MILES. Do not try to cheer me. I am inconsolable!

(COURTESANS *enter from* SENEX'S *house, with a bit of black on their near-nakedness.*)

PSEUDOLUS. Gather around, handmaidens of sorrow.

MILES. (*Sings.*)
Sound the flute,
Blow the horn,
Pluck the lute,
Forward . . . mourn!

(SOLDIERS *and* COURTESANS *wail so effectively that even* HYSTERIUM *is affected.*)

PSEUDOLUS. (*Tragically, over the body.*)
All Crete was at her feet,
All Thrace was in her thrall.
All Sparta loved her sweetness and Gaul . . .
And Spain . . .

MILES.
And Greece . . .

PSEUDOLUS.
And Egypt . . .

MILES.
And Syria . . .

94

PSEUDOLUS.

And Mesopotamia . . .

MOURNERS.

All Crete was at her feet,
All Thrace was in her thrall.
Oh, why should such a blossom fall?

(COURTESANS *pound on bench, frightening* HYSTERIUM, *who falls to the floor.* HE *scrambles back on bench, lies there, his arms unfolded.*)

MILES.

Speak the spells,
Chant the charms,
Toll the bells,

PSEUDOLUS.

Fold the arms!

(HYSTERIUM *slowly folds his arms.*)

Sir, on behalf of the body, I want to thank you for a lovely funeral. I don't know about you, but I've suffered enough. If you will just give me the contract, I shall take the body and . . .

MILES. (*Paying him no attention.*)
Strew the soil,
Strum the lyre,
Spread the oil,
Build the pyre!

PSEUDOLUS. A pyre? What kind of pyre?

MILES. A pyre of fire!

PSEUDOLUS. Oh, a fire pyre!

MILES. She must be burned!

PSEUDOLUS. Burned? Sir . . .

95

MILES. I want her ashes!

PSEUDOLUS. Captain, I implore you. It is not for us to destroy such loveliness. The Gods are awaiting her. They would not be happy if we sent up a smoked virgin!

MILES. I cannot afford to offend the Gods.

PSEUDOLUS. Who can?

MILES. (*Sings.*)
All Crete was at her feet,
But I shall weep no more.
I'll find my consolation as before
Among the simple pleasures of war!

Bring me the contract. (SOLDIER *hands him contract.*) I give her to the gods. (*Puts contract on* HYSTERIUM.) Take her then and lay her to rest. And I shall go my melancholy way. Men. (*Starts to go, stops.*) Wait. A farewell kiss.

PSEUDOLUS. Of course. (*Kisses* MILES *on the cheek.*)

MILES. Not you! (*Pushes him aside, bends over* HYSTERIUM.)

PSEUDOLUS. Sir! You mustn't!

MILES. Why not?

PSEUDOLUS. It could make you very sick. The truth is, she died of an illness contracted on Crete.

MILES. What illness?

PSEUDOLUS. The plague!

(*There is general pandemonium.* COURTESANS *scream "The plague, the plague!" run about wildly, exiting in all directions.*)

MILES. Silence!

PSEUDOLUS. The plague! The plague! Run for your lives! (*To audience.*) Don't just sit there! Run!

96

(MILES *grabs* PSEUDOLUS.)

MILES. There is no plague!

PSEUDOLUS. What?

MILES. I have returned this day from Crete, and there is no plague.

PSEUDOLUS. Then what was everyone yelling about?

(LYCUS *enters, hides behind pillar.*)

MILES. This girl is alive!

HYSTERIUM. (*Jumps up.*) And she's going to stay that way! (*Runs off.*)

MILES. Stop! After her, men! (SOLDIERS *run off.*)

PSEUDOLUS. I'll get her! (*Runs off in opposite direction.*)

MILES. Wait! (*Chases* PSEUDOLUS.)

LYCUS. Now *all* the courtesans have escaped. Eunuchs! I stand to lose a fortune in flesh! (EUNUCH *enters from* LYCUS' *house.*) Find the girls! Bring them back! (EUNUCH *exits, chattering.* LYCUS *exits.* HYSTERIUM *re-enters, hiding face with leafy branch.*)

HYSTERIUM. I've got to get out of these clothes!

(SENEX *enters from* ERRONIUS' *house, spots* HYSTERIUM, *goes to him.*)

SENEX. Ah, there you are, my little dove! (*Cooing.*) You don't have to be afraid of me. (*Leads* HYSTERIUM *to bench, seats him on his lap.*) My slave has prepared a little feast. I want you to serve it to me in there. (*Points to* ERRONIUS' *house.*) Do you understand? Go, then.

(HYSTERIUM *exits into* SENEX'S *house.* SENEX *exits into* ERRONIUS' *house, singing "Everybody Ought to Have a Maid."* HYSTERIUM *pokes his head out of door and ducks*

back into house as HE *sees* EUNUCH *enter with* VIBRATA.
EUNUCH *pushes her into* LYCUS' *house, exits, chattering.*
HYSTERIUM *starts out of house once more as* PSEUDOLUS
runs on, kicks him from behind.)

HYSTERIUM. Pseudolus!

PSEUDOLUS. I ought to give you worse than that! What did you
do with the contract?

HYSTERIUM. I lost it.

PSEUDOLUS. You find it or you're going to get one of the
great beatings of all time!

MILES' VOICE. (*Offstage.*) He dies!

PSEUDOLUS. Look out! (PSEUDOLUS *and* HYSTERIUM *run off in
opposite directions.* MILES *runs on, runs off after* HYSTER-
IUM, *shouting.*)

MILES. This way, men! I have found her!

(SOLDIER *enters and runs off.* DOMINA *enters, disguised
as virgin, removes veil from her face, addresses audience.*)

DOMINA. If it's a pretty face he wants . . . (PSEUDOLUS *enters behind her, gives her a swift kick. She screams.* HE
exits, LYCUS *enters.*) How dare you! (SHE *slaps* LYCUS.)

SOLDIER'S VOICE. (*Offstage.*) Here she is! Men, the virgin!

(SOLDIER *runs on, chases* DOMINA *and* LYCUS *off.* EUNUCH
enters with PANACEA *and* TINTINABULA, *pushes them into*
LYCUS' *house.* HE *exits, chattering.* MILES *enters, as*
DOMINA *re-enters.*)

MILES. My virgin!

DOMINA. Sir, I am not anybody's virgin!

MILES. So you told me! (HE *runs off.* HYSTERIUM *runs on, behind* DOMINA.)

HYSTERIUM. The cause of it all! (*Kicks* DOMINA *in the rear,* SHE *screams,* HE *hides behind pillar, as* LYCUS *runs on.*)

DOMINA. You, again! (*Swings at* LYCUS, *misses, chases him off.* HYSTERIUM *runs to* LYCUS' *house.*)

HYSTERIUM. I have to get out of these clothes!

(SENEX *enters from* ERRONIUS' *house.*)

SENEX. No, no, my dear. Wrong house. (*Chases* HYSTERIUM *around his house.*)

HYSTERIUM. (*As* HE *comes around the first time.*) Leave me alone!

SENEX. (*Following him on the run.*) Ah, you're beautiful when you're angry!

(HERO *appears on balcony of* SENEX'S *house, calls.*)

HERO. Philia! Philia! (*Exits into house.* HYSTERIUM *re-appears from behind* SENEX'S *house.*)

HYSTERIUM. Second time around!

(*Exits into* SENEX'S *house.* PSEUDOLUS *runs on, chased by* SOLDIERS. PSEUDOLUS *leads them among the pillars, swings doors open, knocks two of them out and into the wings, trips* THIRD SOLDIER *who falls.* PSEUDOLUS *runs to him, takes contract from his belt.* HERO *appears on balcony.*)

HERO. All is lost?

PSEUDOLUS. All is won! The contract!—This is what you must do—

(HERO *exits into house, as* MILES *runs on, sword drawn.* PSEUDOLUS *cowers.*)

MILES. You die! (LYCUS *runs on.*) The leper!

LYCUS. Unclean! Unclean!

(MILES *and* PSEUDOLUS *run off in opposite directions.* LYCUS *runs off.* SENEX *appears on roof of his house, coos.*)

SENEX. I know you're up here somewhere, my dear. Philia! Philia! (HE *disappears from roof as* PHILIA *enters from behind* SENEX'S *house.*)

PHILIA. I thought I heard someone call my name. (*Exits into* SENEX'S *house.* TWO EUNUCHS *enter carrying* GEMINAE. ALL *exit into* LYCUS' *house.* DOMINA *enters, hides behind pillar as* PSEUDOLUS, *disguised as eunuch, enters, chattering, leading* GYMNASIA, *exits with her into* LYCUS' *house.*)

DOMINA. That is where my husband is! (*Knocks on* LYCUS' *door.*) I know what goes on in there!

(PSEUDOLUS *appears in upper window of* LYCUS' *house.*)

PSEUDOLUS. Who doesn't?!

(DOMINA *goes to* SENEX'S *house, cautiously looks around. Unseen by her,* HYSTERIUM *enters from same house, looks around, then* PHILIA *also enters from house, looking about.* THEY *just miss seeing each other as* THEY *go in and out of house. Suddenly they see one another, scream and run behind* SENEX'S *house.* PSEUDOLUS *enters from* LYCUS' *house, runs to* SENEX'S *house, opens door. As* PHILIA *runs on from behind house,* HE *pushes her through the doorway. As* HYSTERIUM *passes,* PSEUDOLUS *kicks him and* HYSTERIUM *tumbles into* ERRONIUS' *house.* DOMINA *chases after* HYSTERIUM. SHE *is followed by* SENEX *who catches her at* ERRONIUS' *door, pushes her in, triumphantly.*)

SENEX. At last!

(HERO *re-appears on balcony.*)

PSEUDOLUS. Hero! The contract! (*Throws contract to him.*) To the harbor!

HERO. What will happen to you?

PSEUDOLUS. Nothing. Here is what I will do. I shall cause a diversion. Then I shall drink a potion which will make me appear as if dead.

(HERO *exits into house.* DOMINA *enters from* ERRONIUS' *house, followed by* SENEX. PSEUDOLUS *ducks into* SENEX'S *house.*)

DOMINA. Dearest Senex, you saw through my disguise!

SENEX. Yes, beloved. (SHE *embraces him.* HE *looks around for* PHILIA.)

DOMINA. Forgive me for mistrusting you. My darling, it's just that you have been a little distant these last twenty-nine years.

SENEX. (*Backing off.*) Yes, beloved, yes. (*Exits, as* SHE *follows.*)

DOMINA. Senex! Senex!

ERRONIUS. (*Entering.*) Third time around! (*Starts for his house, as* HYSTERIUM *is entering from same house. Seeing* ERRONIUS, HE *runs* back in.) The spirit! (*Sneaks over to side of his house.* HYSTERIUM *peeks out of door, then tiptoes out, not seeing* ERRONIUS.) Who are you?! (HYSTERIUM *trips and falls.* ERRONIUS *helps him up.*) Let me help you.

HYSTERIUM. Thank you. I am quite all right.

ERRONIUS. (*Seeing ring.*) Wait!

HYSTERIUM. What is it?

ERRONIUS. My dear one! My sweet one! My little one! (*Kisses* HYSTERIUM.)

HYSTERIUM. Why do older men find me so attractive?

101

ERRONIUS. My daughter!

HYSTERIUM. What?

ERRONIUS. You wear the ring with the gaggle of geese!

HYSTERIUM. I am not your daughter!

(MILES *and* THREE SOLDIERS *run on, spot* HYSTERIUM.)

MILES. There she is!

ERRONEUS. Yes!

MILES. My virgin!

HYSTERIUM. I am not a virgin!

ERRONIUS. Those filthy pirates!

HYSTERIUM. I am not your daughter! I . . . uh . . . I am an Etruscan dancer. (*Dances a few steps as* SENEX *re-enters.*)

SENEX. Dancing with impatience, my dear?

MILES. Who is it speaks so boldly to my virgin?

SENEX. Your what? She is my maid!

ERRONIUS. She is my daughter!

(ALL *tug at* HYSTERIUM.)

HYSTERIUM. Please! No fighting! That hurts! Please! (*In the tussle, without knowing it,* HYSTERIUM *loses his wig.*)

MILES. You are not the virgin!

HYSTERIUM. (*Walks into* ERRONIUS' *arms.*) Of course not! I am this old man's baby daughter.

SENEX. Hysterium!

MILES. The eunuch!

ERRONIUS. My daughter is a eunuch?

102

MILES. Seize that man! (*Points to* HYSTERIUM. SOLDIERS *point swords at him.*)

DOMINA. (*Entering.*) Senex!

MILES. You, again?

SENEX. Sir, you are speaking to my wife!

MILES. You are married to that . . . that . . .

SENEX. Yes, I am married to that . . . that! And I shall thank you to release my slave and remove yourself from in front of my house!

MILES. Your house? This is the house of Lycus.

DOMINA. Lycus?

(ALL *babble.*)

MILES. Quiet! I declare this area under martial law!

PSEUDOLUS. (*Entering from* SENEX'S *house and indicating* HYSTERIUM.) Release that man!

MILES. Release that man! (*Recognizes* PSEUDOLUS.) You!

PSEUDOLUS. Sir, this quivering creature is blameless. It is I, and I alone, who have caused you this grief.

MILES. Men, unseize him and seize him! (SOLDIERS *surround* PSEUDOLUS.) And now, death by evisceration!

(PSEUDOLUS *reacts horribly.*)

HYSTERIUM. Oh, Pseudolus!

PSEUDOLUS. Calm, my friend. Sir, I believe a doomed man is allowed a final request?

MILES. Yes.

PSEUDOLUS. Allow me to take my own life.

MILES. Sir, I have seen kings with less courage.

103

PSEUDOLUS. So have I. Hysterium, the potion. You know the one I mean.

HYSTERIUM. The potion? (*Picks up cup from where* HE *placed it earlier.*)

PSEUDOLUS. Thank you, dear friend. Give the hemlock to Socrates.

HYSTERIUM. (*To* SOLDIERS.) Which one of you is Socrates?

PSEUDOLUS. Give me that! (*Takes cup, raises it.*) I go to sail on uncharted seas. To the harbor, *to the harbor* . . . (PHILIA *and* HERO *sneak out of* SENEX'S *house, exit unseen.*) . . . from which no mariner returns. Farewell. (*Drains potion, dies noisily and elaborately.* MILES *leans over him.*) Kiss me! (*Jumps up.*) Somebody kiss me! Anybody! (*To* HYSTERIUM.) I could kill you . . . you darling!

MILES. Seize him! (SOLDIER *grabs* PSEUDOLUS.)

PSEUDOLUS. Thank you! I needed that!

MILES. Stop that! (*Smacks* PSEUDOLUS *in back of head.*)

(LYCUS *enters with* PHILIA. HERO *follows.*)

LYCUS. Great Miles Gloriosus! I would not reveal my true identity until I could deliver that which I had promised. Sir, I am Lycus. Philia, go to the man who bought you.

(PHILIA *sighs, goes to* SENEX. DOMINA *reacts.*)

SENEX. No, no.

PHILIA. Aren't you the . . . ?

SENEX. Quiet! We're under martial law.

LYCUS. *There* is the captain! Captain, here is your virgin.

MILES. And worth the waiting for. (*To* PSEUDOLUS.) Out of the great joy of the occasion, forgiveness. You are free.

PSEUDOLUS. Free . . . to be a slave. (*Slumps against pillar.*)

ERRONIUS. I cannot understand it. There was the ring. The ring with the gaggle of geese.

MILES. What did you say, old man? (MILES *extends his hand.*)

ERRONIUS. The ring!

MILES. Father!

ERRONIUS. You've grown! (THEY *embrace.*)

PHILIA. (*Showing ring on chain about her neck.*) Are these many geese a gaggle?

ERRONIUS. How long have you had this?

PHILIA. I've had this since, I don't know when I've had this since.

ERRONIUS. My daughter!

MILES. My sister?!

HYSTERIUM. Pseudolus, did you hear that?

PSEUDOLUS. Silence! Stand back, everyone! My dear old man, I take it your daughter is free born?

ERRONIUS. Without a doubt!

PSEUDOLUS. Lycus, as all of us know, the penalty for selling a free-born citizen is to be trampled to death by a water buffalo in heat!

MILES. Seize him!

LYCUS. Careful, I'm a bleeder!

PSEUDOLUS. (*To* LYCUS.) Bring out those girls! (*To audience.*) I told you this was to be a comedy! (*As* LYCUS *brings* COURTESANS *out of his house.*) Hero!

HERO. Mother and father, I wish to marry.

105

SENEX. (*Aside.*) Son, if you are only as happy as your mother and I, my heart will bleed for you.

PSEUDOLUS. (*Sings, to audience, indicating* HERO *and* PHILIA.)
Lovers divided
Get coincided.
Something for everyone:

HERO *and* PHILIA.
A comedy tonight!

PSEUDOLUS. (*Indicating* SENEX *and* DOMINA.)
Father and mother
Get one another.

DOMINA.
Something for everyone:

SENEX.
A tragedy tonight!

MILES. (*Holding the* GEMINAE.)
I get the twins!
They get the best!

ERRONIUS.
I get a family . . .

HYSTERIUM.
I get a rest.

SOLDIERS. (*Holding the other* COURTESANS.)
We get a few girls.

LYCUS.
I'll get some new girls.

PSEUDOLUS.
I get the thing I want to be:
Free!

ALL.
Free! Free! Free! Free! Free!

(PSEUDOLUS *exits joyfully*)

Nothing for kings,
Nothing for crowns,
Something for lovers, liars and clowns!
What is the moral?
Must be a moral.
Here is the moral, wrong or right:

PSEUDOLUS. (*Re-enters with* GYMNASIA.)
Morals tomorrow!

ALL.
Comedy tonight!

CURTAIN